1997

ALCOHOLISM AND PASTORAL MINISTRY: READINGS ON RECOVERY

Steven L. Berg, Ph.D.
Editor

Guest House, Inc.
Lake Orion, Michigan

1989

Guest House, Inc.
1840 W. Scripps Road
Lake Orion, MI 48035

LORAIN AND JUDY BERG
G.C. LANDON

and to the memory of

AUSTIN RIPLEY

ACKNOWLEDGEMENTS

I used to think that the editors of anthologies had easy jobs because all they had to do was rely on other peoples' work. Yet, I have found that editing, like writing original material, is time consuming and is best done in collaboration with others.

While editing <u>Alcoholism and Pastoral Ministry</u> I had the privilege to work with three supportive communities. First, there was a group of people at Guest House. LuAnn Beamer did most of the clerical work associated with this book and Nancy Meyer, our computer expert, designed the page layout and graciously did more than her share by seeing that the manuscript was correctly formatted. Dr. Ernest Kurtz, Joelma Moore, and Pamela Jozwik completed the team in Research and Education. Michael Goddard, John Gumina, and Dotti Taylor each lent their support.

But of the people at Guest House, I am especially grateful to Richard J. Koehn who put his faith in the "Bibliography Project on Spiritual Issues in Recovery" even before there was an official project. Early in 1987, Mr. Koehn said that if we started a bibliography project, a possible outcome might be a manual on pastoral ministry. It is a tribute to his dedication and leadership that Guest House not only has a database and library on spirituality in recovery, but that the first publication from this project is a book on pastoral ministry. This book, in part, is dedicated to the memory of Austin Ripley, founder of Guest House. But a living tribute to Austin Ripley is seen each day in the work of Mr. Koehn.

The second community of support was from Michigan State University and the Lansing metropolitan area. I am especially grateful to Jacque Shoppell who not only served as proof reader, but, more importantly, as dear friend and colleague. George C. Landon has, for years, served as a role model and friend. There was also a great deal of support from those known as the "Back Porch Group."

Finally, family is another important community. I wish to thank my brothers Christopher and Mike, sister-in-law Janice, nephew Alex and grandmother Rachael Liberacki, Frank Scheer, Valerie Przywara, Marty Carlson, Andrew Stuart, Harvey Ballard, Barbara Harte, Mary Hartshorn, David Smith and Dan Krantz. I especially want to thank my parents, Lorain and Judy Berg, who taught me that you don't need to be ordained to practice pastoral ministry. This book is dedicated to them.

INTRODUCTION

While it is impossible for members of the clergy to avoid alcohol and other drug problems, it is equally unrealistic to expect a priest, nun, minister, or rabbi to have the time to sort through the proliferation of recent publications on addiction. Addiction is a serious problem, but it is not the only problem faced by members of the clergy.

Alcoholism and Pastoral Ministry is both an anthology and resource guide designed for the pastoral minister who wants to know more about alcoholism. The articles chosen are meant to provide an overview of alcoholism, including ministering to alcoholics and their families.

Quite often books which attempt to be too universal fail to effectively reach any audience, so we decided this anthology would focus on issues relating to what we do best at Guest House -- rehabilitating Catholic priests, brothers, and seminarians. As a result, the essays chosen for Alcoholism and Pastoral Ministry are geared for a predominately Catholic audience. However, we did not feel compelled to choose articles which only addressed Catholics.

Over the years, tremendous advances have been made in the treatment field. Because these advances are best understood in their historical context, chapter one includes selections on AA history and the history of religious attitudes toward alcohol and alcoholism.

Chapter two contains stories from recovered alcoholics. In making our selections, we made an effort to show the diversity of experience among alcoholics. Another source for stories is Alcoholics Anonymous, the basic text of AA (also known as "The Big Book").

The essays selected for chapter three illustrate the role which spirituality plays in the recovery process. By addressing the spiritual component of recovery, alcoholics can avoid becoming "non-drinking, non-recovered alcoholics."

In addition to pointing out the special skills which members of the clergy have for working with alcoholics, the essays in chapter four were chosen to help pastoral ministers better understand why some individuals affected by alcoholism have difficulty confiding in them. These essays should help readers gain new confidence in their abilities as well as a better understanding of the types of referrals they can make.

The essays in chapter five concern diversity. The progression of alcoholism is fairly uniform from one alcoholic to the next, but the experiences of individual alcoholics vary dramatically. Ministers who can address specific needs of the individual are better able to assist spiritual growth. Although this chapter is devoted to the topic, issues of diversity appear throughout the book.

Because members of the clergy are not immune to alcoholism, chapter six contains essays which relate to its central theme, "What happens when the spiritual leader is spiritually sick?" There are also articles concerning religious communities who need to confront the issue of alcoholism in one of their members.

At the end of each chapter is a list of suggestions for further readings. To request additional information, please write to: Research and Education Department, Guest House, 1840 W. Scripps Road, Lake Orion, MI 48035.

Steven L. Berg, Ph.D.
Coordinator
Bibliography Project on
Spiritual Issues in Recovery

ALCOHOLISM AND PASTORAL MINISTRY: READINGS ON RECOVERY

Table of Contents

Ministry to Alcoholics

Diversity Among Alcoholics

Alcoholic Clergy

wife Lois in a blue side car, he toured the Northeast, making confidential reports on the status of various small business enterprises. The drive for success was on.

Inevitably, Bill became involved in the stock market itself; business and financial leaders were his heroes. For several years Wall Street brought him money and applause. He and his charming Lois made an ever-widening circle of friends, and their style of living left nothing to be desired-- superficially, that is. But all along, drinking was assuming a more important place, soon continuing all day and frequently most of the night. His friends and his young wife remonstrated. But many around him were getting rich, so "why not I?" thought Bill, liquor and all.

Then abruptly in October, 1929, all hell broke loose on the New York Stock Exchange, and the effect on Bill proved catastrophic. Here's the picture as he used to tell it at Gramercy Park:

After a seething day he would wobble from brokerage office to hotel bar and back again and find the ticker tape still clattering tardily about eight. Grabbing a strip, he would stare at an inch which read ABC-19. It might have been 54 that morning. Like most of his friends, he was soon finished. The evening papers were reporting more than one instance of a Wall Street leader hurling himself to death from some "tower of high finance," but such cowardice disgusted Bill. Tomorrow was another day. When drinking again at a bar, the old fierce determination to win always came back with overwhelming force.

One morning he phoned a friend in Montreal. Apparently there was still plenty of money in Canada, and by the following spring Lois and he were living north of the border and again in their accustomed style.

For awhile Bill felt like Napoleon freed from Elba, but not for long. On his travels his drinking problem stuck right

with him. One generous friend after another had to let him
go, and quite soon the Wilsons were again living in Brooklyn
and broke. This time they stayed broke.

They found sanctuary with Lois' parents and she took a
job as a salesgirl in a Manhattan department store, often
reaching home exhausted to find Bill dead drunk. As for
Bill, he had become an unwilling hanger-on in brokerage
offices. He also loitered more and more at home where the
liquor, which from a luxury had turned into a necessity, cost
less. Remorse, hopelessness, even horror marked the next
several years. His old courage to do battle had evaporated.
Eating little or nothing when drinking, Bill was soon forty
pounds underweight.

One short respite came after a visit to a nationally
known New York hospital for the rehabilitation of
alcoholics. He had been sent there through the interest of
his brother-in-law, a physician. A kind doctor, William D.
Silkworth, who became his lifelong friend, not only explained
how seriously ill he was but how (and why) his will power
had become incapable of combating liquor. Bill felt that this
partially excused his incredible behavior, so he returned to
the Street and was soon making a little money again. But
self-knowledge alone failed miserably to answer his problems,
and the awful days of the drinking bouts returned all too
soon. His family saw the undertaker or an asylum ahead,
and Bill's loneliness turned into despair.

Meanwhile, on Gramercy Park, along with much personal
work or personal counseling, various forces, including Sam
Shoemaker's keen interest in programs for laymen, had
encouraged the formation of midweek men's meetings
characteristic of "A First Century Christian Fellowship," or
"The Oxford Group," as this movement was now being
called. In many of these weekly groups Christ's promise to
His followers, that where two or three of them might gather

in His name, He would personally be present, was being fulfilled. The meetings were lively and spiritually effective. The one held late in the afternoon every Thursday used an attractive, conveniently located lounge on the second floor of "61" and was presided over by an experienced member of the Calvary staff, or a leader in the wider fellowship, who knew the kind of questions businessmen and wage earners needed to air and discuss: answers to pressure, personal hang-ups, honesty in competitive business dealings, fear, or unemployment.

In God's own time and through a friend's rather casual visit to this group, the first gleam of hope was relayed to Bill. One bleak November afternoon Bill's phone rang. His old boarding-school friend and drinking companion, Ebby Thatcher, was on the other end of the wire. What surprised Bill was not so much that Ebby was in town but that he was sober, and when he arrived at the family residence in Brooklyn, he seemed strangely different from the hopeless man Bill had known. On the kitchen table stood a crock of pineapple juice and gin. Bill filled a glass and pushed it across as they sat down opposite each other. But smilingly Ebby refused.

Bill wondered what it was all about, but not for long. "I've got religion," volunteered Ebby without the slightest inhibition.

"Oh, not that!" Bill gulped a double mouthful of his brew. Then he sat glumly thinking there was nothing he could do but let his friend rant. Instead, Ebby related a short, moving story about two friends who, interceded in his favor several months before, had persuaded a New England judge to suspend sentence on a conviction in a case resulting from a brawl. They had professed faith in him, came up with a specific program of action--and it had worked.

Bill pretended to be unimpressed, but the story and especially Ebby's smile spoke to him eloquently. After all, he had always claimed to believe in a Power greater than himself. "What do you call this brand of religion?" he heard himself asking.

Ebby pretended to be tantalizingly vague. He mentioned an old church down on Gramercy Park and the friendliness shown him by men who met there week by week. "They're a great crowd," he added, "with some fresh ideas. They admit alcohol has 'em licked, so why shouldn't I? As one of them put it, 'Love's blind but the neighbors ain't!' When I took stock of myself the result was awful; but when I spilled the beans, confidentially, to another souse I felt like a new man. I also got some helpful thoughts about making a bit of what they call 'restitution.' I was told that there was no price tag on giving--if it's just giving yourself. And again it worked."

This time Bill, his long legs stretched out across the kitchen floor, was silent.

Ebby didn't stay long and he had no clincher, but he spoke quite seriously about a new experiment in prayer with which he was now starting every day. "Free as the air, too, Bill," he said, "because you only have to pray to God **as you think He is.**"

What could be fairer than that? Bill got the distinct impression that his friend was no longer fighting a drinking problem. No, the desire to imbibe had somehow just been lifted and he was asking daily for the power, not to struggle against alcohol but to live a life. Obviously he was finding it.

For several days Bill continued to mix his gin and fruit juice but he simply couldn't forget Ebby, not for a single waking moment. He felt rocked and stunned, but rather happily so. Ebby had not talked down to him nor given much advice. He felt the closeness of the old days in a fresh way. As he put it later, here was the kinship of common suffering and the enormously powerful influence of the simple fact of **one alcoholic talking to another.**

Viewed in the golden retrospect of the years to come this amounted to "round one" in Bill's fight for freedom.

In making him rector, Calvary Church had put several unexpected assets into Sam Shoemaker's hands, and none that he was to value more than a mission for down-and-outs on East Twenty-third Street. Connected with it was a rooming house called The Olive Tree Inn. Presided over by Harry Hadley and "Tex" Francisco, Calvary Mission provided evening meetings and simple meals, a place to sleep, and, for those who were finding freedom from liquor, a warm fellowship for hopeless men. Since he totally lacked resources, Ebby had gone there to live. With the men he met, and with the new friends in nearby Gramercy Park, he now enjoyed an ever-increasing number of close relationships.

Bill knew where Ebby was and one day, between his mood swings and while still "pretty maudlin," he got the bright idea of doing a bit of religious investigation by paying Ebby a call. Unfortunately, it was a long walk from the nearest subway station to Calvary Mission and Bill began stopping in bars as he traveled east on Twenty-third Street. Most of the afternoon slipped by between drinks and he was in high fettle in a drunken way by the time he finally reached the mission's front door. He had picked up a Finnish sailmaker and this unruly pair were on the point of being refused admission when Ebby himself appeared, quickly appraised the situation, and suggested a plate of beans. After the food had been washed down with copious cups of black coffee, the newcomers heard there would

shortly be a meeting in the mission hall. Would they like to
go? Certainly, they said, that was why they were there.

Sitting on one of the hard wooden pews that filled the
hall, Bill shivered at the sight of the derelict audience.
There followed a few hymns and prayers and then an
exhortation by Tex, the evening's leader. Only Jesus could
save, he said, and strangely enough his words failed to jar.
Whatever he meant, Bill felt he must be right. He listened
with rising excitement as certain men got up and gave
testimonials. Then came "the call." As various men started
forward, Bill found himself, unaccountably motivated,
heading for the altar. Ebby grabbed for his coattails but it
was too late. He knelt, shaking the more, among the
penitents and felt, perhaps for the first time, truly penitent
himself. He had a wild impulse to talk and this he did with
deep earnestness and in a way that compelled attention.

Afterwards, sitting in the dormitory in the building next
door, where Ebby was living, he could remember scarcely a
word he had said. Ebby, obviously relieved, told him he had
done all right and had "given his life to God."

This experience may be called "round two."

When he reached home Bill gave a full account of his
experience to Lois, and they had a long and earnest talk. It
seemed significant to both of them that on his return trip
along Twenty-third Street he had never once thought of
going to a bar. This was something very new!

Came the dawn, and Bill realized that he had slept like
a baby and without an ounce of gin. He had only a slight
hangover, not the devastating head he had expected. But
his old habits still gripped him. He would not be a fanatic
about this new life. He would take another drink or two
just by way of tapering off.

When Lois had left for work, the process became easier,
and instead of tapering off he took a couple more and

nicely succeeded in tapering **on**. At six o'clock his wife found him upstairs on the bed and, of course, drunk.

So it went for two grim days; but Ebby's smile and the mission experience never left him. On the morning of the third day his wandering thoughts gathered into a sharp focus as he began to compare himself to a victim of cancer. Surely if he had cancer he would not sit at home and put cold cream on the affected parts. Certainly not! He would look up the best doctor in the business and put himself unreservedly into his hands. So now he would return to the hospital and his old friend Dr. Silkworth. Here at least he would be helped to sober up, and then perhaps he could take a fresh look at Ebby's formula for sobriety.

He arrived at the hospital in wretched shape, having consumed two bottles of beer en route. According to all accounts, Dr. Silkworth met him in the hall. In very high spirits Bill waved a third bottle in the doctor's face, and yelled, "At last, Doc, I've found something!" At this the good doctor's face fell, and Bill realized all the more how deeply the medical man loved him. The doctor merely shook his head and intimated that it might be time for Bill to get upstairs and into bed.

Some three days passed. The effects of both the alcohol and the sedatives he had been given wore off. In their place Bill suffered a dull sense of emptiness and depression. As he put it, he was "still choking on the God business." Then, bright and early one morning he saw Ebby's smiling face before him again, Ebby in person. Ah, thought Bill, here's where he thinks he's going to evangelize me. He waited suspiciously but nothing happened except that Ebby entered the room and sat down.

Finally it was Bill who spoke. "What's that neat little formula once more?" he asked. In perfect good humor Ebby recited the group precepts again. You admit you are licked. You get honest with yourself. You talk things out with somebody else. If possible you make restitution to the people you have harmed. You try to give of yourself without stint and with no demand for reward. And you pray to whatever God you think there is, entirely as an experiment. It was as simple and as mysterious as that.

After some small talk, Ebby again vanished. Bill's depression deepened unbearably. It seemed to him as though he were now at the very bottom of the pit. He still gagged badly on the notion of approaching that "Power greater than yourself," but the last vestige of his pride and obstinacy had been crushed.

Then quite suddenly he found himself crying out, "If there is a God, let Him show Himself. I am ready to do anything, **anything**!

At this the whole room lit up with a great light reminiscent of the Spirit of Christmas Present in Dickens' A Christmas Carol. Bill could only describe it by saying that he had been caught up in an ecstasy. In his mind's eye he saw himself on the top of a high mountain with the wind of the Spirit blowing. The acute sense that burst upon him that he was a free man was crucial.

This proved to be his third and in a sense his final "round."

Slowly his ecstasy subsided, and instead he felt a great peace and a presence which he could only identify as the supernatural Presence of the Living God. No matter how terrible the past had been, of one thing he was sure--the future was to be all right for it was to be with Him.

When Dr. Silkworth next stopped in, Bill tried to give him an account of his astonishing experience. He feared the doctor might feel that he was hallucinating or losing his mind. But the reverse proved to be the doctor's attitude. He immediately encouraged Bill to hold on to the reality of all he had gone through. "You're by no means going crazy," he said. "Some basic psychological or spiritual event has happened. Hang on to it. **Anything** is better than the way you were."

Then faithful Ebby called again, this time with a worn copy of Varieties of Religious Experience by the great Harvard psychologist, William James. Together they devoured parts of it. Spiritual experiences, James had written, were gifts from the blue but they could transform people. Often they were preceded by pain, suffering, or calamity. Complete hopelessness and "deflation at depth" were almost always part of the picture. Bill took it all personally, for this was his own history, especially the realization that deflation at depth had ushered in the spiritual renewal and freedom he now felt.

Before the day was out he was already focused on changing the world, and when he was dismissed from the hospital, he started out after drunks like a person on jet propulsion. He envisioned a chain reaction that would dry up the nation. But actually his next necessary lesson was the old adage that patience is a virtue.

As part of the new life, he threw himself into group activity both at Calvary House and Calvary Mission. He took on alcoholics by the score; some would clear up for a little while but then flop dismally. Bill maintained his own sobriety, however, but at the end of six months nobody else had become sober for long. Unfortunately he wasn't meeting men at their own point of need, as Ebby had done for him. Instead he was trying to impose Robert E. Speer's four "absolute standards" from the Sermon on the Mount. These standards, that had often been used so wisely by Oxford Group leaders and others on people who were physically sick and mentally obsessed, were now backfiring.

Dr. Silkworth was one of the first to underline Bill's mistaken approach. "You're **preaching** at these fellows, Bill," he said, in essence, "although no one ever preached at you. Turn your strategy around. Remember Professor James's insistence that 'deflation at great depth' is the foundation of most spiritual experiences like your own. Give your new contacts the **medical** business--and hard. Describe the obsession that condemns men to drink and the physical sensitivity or allergy of the body that makes this type go mad or die if they keep on drinking."

Bill saw the point and heartily agreed. However, not a little pressure continued to be brought on him by some of his new friends who wanted him to forget his alcoholics and get on with "changing the world." For his part, Bill knew that he was being called to go for something more specific, and that more than anything else he wanted to work with alcoholics. In this Sam Shoemaker remained a staunch ally, for despite his immersion in both group and parish work, Sam well remembered his own single failure with the few drunks to whom he had given rooms in Calvary House instead of at The Olive Tree Inn. Who could forget? One of these had gleefully tossed an alarm clock out of a fourth floor window in the dead of night, putting it neatly through a stained-glass window of the church. At early communion the next morning the clergy had suddenly noticed it on the embroidered cloth of the high altar. Sam realized further that the pull on Bill to work with others who were handicapped, as he had been, represented something very special. While he remained just as unclear as Bill as to where and how this "ministry" would finally take root, he strongly shared Bill's desire to explore his true vocation and look for an open door through which he might fulfill it.

Strangely enough Bill's chance came not in New York City but among another crowd of Oxford Group friends in

Akron, Ohio. In looking for work Bill had drifted back to Wall Street again, still completely sober but very frustrated. One day, through a chance acquaintance in a brokerage office, he got himself mixed up in a proxy fight involving a small manufacturing company in the Midwest. He and a few others visited Ohio to look into things. Again in fine fettle, Bill could already see himself as the company's new president; but when the chips were down the other side had more proxies and Bill and his friends got ousted.

At this point everyone but Bill returned to New York. With no more than ten dollars in his pocket, he found himself at the Mayflower Hotel in Akron on the eve of Mother's Day--and alone. As he paced the hotel lobby he could see the bar filling up at one end and hear the familiar buzz of conversation mounting. But God was with him. He recalled clearly that it had always been **by trying to help other alcoholics** that he had stayed sober himself. That was it, he thought. He must find another alcoholic to talk to. Down deep he realized for the first time that he needed that other alcoholic just as much as the man he wanted to help needed him.

Across from the bar at the far end of the lobby he paused by a church directory. Then quite at random he called an Episcopal priest and to his listener's amazement poured out his tale. Finally he asked if the minister knew of someone who could put him in touch with another alcoholic. When the good man realized what Bill was looking for, he may well have envisioned two people getting drunk instead of one. In any event he finally got Bill's point and came up with a list of some ten people who might be able to help.

Still in the phone booth Bill began calling. It was a Saturday afternoon and scarcely anyone was home. One line was busy and the few people who did answer failed to respond. Bill got down to the very last name, but this one did the trick. A young married woman, Henrietta Seiberling, answered. She had no drinking problem herself, she said, but she knew a man, a doctor, who indeed did need help. She suggested that Bill come straight over and pursue things further.

So it was that within twenty-four hours Bill stood face to face with "Dr. Bob" who, with his wife, Anne, had gone to several group meetings in Akron, and who was later to become AA member number two and co-founder with Bill of Alcoholics Anonymous.

Nothing seemed very promising at the time. Dr. Bob and Anne came in. The doctor, visibly shaking, explained that he could only stay for a minute. However their hostess discreetly led the two men to a small library and there they went on talking until after eleven o'clock. Bill kept reminding himself that previously, in New York, his aggressive approach had backfired, so he proceeded carefully, with no mention of the fireworks of his own full-blown religious experience. He bore down on an alcoholic's allergy to liquor and his obsession with drink once he got started. Though Dr. Bob was a medical doctor this was news to him, **bad** news. But here they were, two drunks, face to face, and one of them with an answer. This mutual give-and-take became the very heart of AA in the days to come. As Bill talked the doctor relaxed. "Yes, that's me," he began to say. "I'm like that." They were talking the same language.

As it worked out, Bill went to live with Dr. Bob and Anne. Every morning they experimented in having their devotions together. As Bill described it later, Anne would sit in the corner by the fireplace and read from the Bible, and then they would huddle together in the stillness awaiting inspiration and guidance. The final missing link in Bill's program had been located and new insights were given. Both men felt the immense importance of continuing to work with other alcoholics and, through contacts at the Akron City Hospital, the third and fourth members of AA were reached, helped, and included in their fellowship.

Besides that first Akron group, on Bill's return East, there soon developed a weekly meeting in the Wilson's Brooklyn parlor. When Bill visited Sam Shoemaker, who had been keenly following his progress, the two had a memorable reunion. After a few months, several meeting places opened up, such as a room in New York's Steinway Hall, one in a Manhattan tailoring shop, and others in suburban homes. Gradually groups began to appear in other cities--Philadelphia, Washington, Baltimore, and Cleveland. An AA ferment had begun to work and the good news began to spread rapidly. Today every city in the land and hundreds overseas--one might say almost every hamlet--has its AA group. And the end is never in sight. For alcoholism has become a major illness throughout the world, Praise God that, through the faithfulness and experience of two men, this growing problem has an answer--adequate, effective, and immediately at hand.

The Twelve Steps of Alcoholics Anonymous

According the Lois Wilson, when Bill was writing the "big" AA book in 1938, he thought of his many talks with Dr. Bob about the importance of stressing the spiritual aspect of the program. He therefore expanded the original six steps, which they had learned from the Oxford groups, into the famous Twelve Steps now used around the world. He had a deep desire to make it impossible for an alcoholic who wanted sobriety to find a single loophole. The steps have never since been altered.

Step One: We admitted that we were powerless over alcohol--that our lives had become unmanageable.

Step Two: Came to believe that a Power greater than ourselves could restore us to sanity.

Step Three: Made a decision to turn our will and our lives over to the care of God **as we understood Him.**

Step Four: Made a searching and fearless moral inventory of ourselves.

Step Five: Admitted to God, to ourselves, and to another human being the exact nature of our wrongs.

Step Six: Were entirely ready to have God remove all these defects of character.

Step Seven: Humbly asked Him to remove our shortcomings.

Step Eight: Made a list of all persons we had harmed, and became willing to make amends to them all.

Step Nine: Made direct amends to such people whenever possible, except when to do so would injure them or others.

Step Ten: Continued to take personal inventory and when we were wrong promptly admitted it.

Step Eleven: Sought through prayer and meditation to improve our conscious contact with God **as we**

understood Him, praying only for knowledge of His will for us and the power to carry that out.

Step Twelve: Having had a spiritual awakening as the result of these steps, we tried to carry this message to alcoholics, and to practice these principles in all our affairs.

This originally appeared in The Breeze of the Spirit (New York, New York: The Seabury Press, 1978, 45-56.) It is reprinted with permission.

THE CHURCHES AND ALCOHOL

Rev. Roland H. Bainton

Church attitudes toward alcohol use and the disease of alcoholism vary from denomination to denomination. Furthermore, these attitudes have historic roots. In this essay, Roland H. Bainton distinguishes the differences between Catholic, Protestant, and Jewish reactions to alcohol by setting these attitudes in an historic context.

The motion picture Going My Way offers a striking illustration of the difference between Catholic and Protestant clerical mores as to sex and drink. In the story, a young priest, by a vow of celibacy, wounds a heart. An old priest has concealed in a bookcase, behind the works of General Grant, a whisky flask. A Protestant clergyman would have married the girl, but in many denominations he would never have been able to grow old in the ministry if he were caught with the flask. The Protestant clergyman is expected to be abstinent, the Catholic to be celibate. Of course, each is free to emulate the virtues expected of the other, but the pressures are differently weighted. The Catholic priest is subject to obligatory celibacy. The Protestant clergy is well-nigh subject to obligatory matrimony. Such differences in practice make one wonder whether Protestant rigorism may not be directed to drink and Catholic rigorism to sex.

If this be true, the explanation might be that Catholicism is prevalent among southern peoples more prone to sexual excess, and Protestantism in northern climes more disposed to intemperance in drink. The mores required of the clergy represent, in each case, a recoil against abuses. This explanation, although plausible, is at every step too simple.

To begin with, Catholicism and Protestantism are not to be neatly equated with south and north, for Catholicism has a great hold in Ireland and Poland, and Protestantism was once strong in France. Neither can we be too confident that excess in sex is southern and excess in drink is northern. Statistics for the year 1927 reveal that in the total consumption of alcoholic beverages France was first, Spain second, Italy third and Germany in the twenty-first place.

On the other hand, the generalization may be defensible for the days in which the Catholic and Protestant ethics were formulated. In the time of St. Augustine, who did so much to fashion the Catholic view, the Germanic invaders were reputed to more chaste than the Romans. The Vandals were lauded by the vanquished for having closed the brothels of Carthage, whereas in the period when the Protestant ethic was taking shape at the hands of Martin Luther in Germany, this people was notorious for drunkenness. These considerations perhaps support an explanation ultimately in terms of climate. But this again is too simple. Religious ideas mould conduct even in defiance of climate.

A more serious difficulty is that the lines do not fall neatly between Protestant and Catholic on the matter of drink. The Lutheran and the Anglican churches on this point have preserved the Catholic attitude. Not even Puritanism in its formative period espoused total abstinence and prohibition. The initiative came from the Methodists and Quakers, with the churches of the Puritan tradition rallying to their support. If one would understand how all this came to be, a little historical sketch of the attitude of the churches toward the consumption of alcoholic beverages is in order.

The Jewish Attitude

The starting point must be the attitude of Judaism, which was taken over by the early Church, as to the use of fermented drinks. This attitude was conditioned by the essential character of Jewish religion, which is neither ascetic nor orgiastic. The former type repudiates drink altogether along with all the delights of life. The latter utilizes drink in order to stimulate religious emotion. Ascetic religions regard the material world as evil and seek whenever possible to avoid contact with matter. They commonly proscribe contacts with women, war and wine, because sexual relations, killing and intoxication are all defiling. Of this attitude there is scarcely a trace in the Old Testament. Judaism is an affirmative religion. God created the world and saw that it was good. The Psalmist praises the Lord for "He causeth the grass to grow for the cattle and herb for the service of man...and wine that maketh glad the heart of man" (Ps 104: 13-15).

Judaism, on the other hand, is not an orgiastic nature religion, discovering particular evidence of the divine in the process of fertilization, vegetation and fermentation and seeking communion with God through the excitements of sex and drink. This type of religion was found in Canaan in the Baal cult, and in the Hellenistic world in the rites of Dionysus. Against all such orgies the prophets of Israel were flint, even to the point of slaughtering the priests of Baal. Drunkenness in Judaism, whether connected or unconnected with religion, met with the sternest rebuke. Noah, Lot and Nabal were subjected to reprobation for their lapses. Incidentally, one of the problems for Biblical commentators has been to explain how Noah could be sober for 601 years and then get drunk. The classical denunciations of drunkenness in the Old Testament are to be found in the Book of Proverbs: "Wine is a mocker and strong drink a brawler...Look not upon the wine when it is red, when it sparkleth in the cup, when it goeth down smoothly: at the last it biteth like a serpent and stingeth like an adder" (Prov. 20:1 and 23:31).

The only cure for drunkenness contemplated in the Old Testament is moderation. We do hear, however, of two groups of total abstainers, the Nazirites and the Rechabites. The Nazirites, in the interest of holiness, vowed to hold themselves aloof for a limited period from razors, corpses and wine (Num. 6: 1-6). Here, there is a suggestion of ascetic religion. In the case of the Rechabites abstinence was a survival of nomadic mores. The Israelites, before their invasion of Canaan, had been desert tribes for whom liquor was difficult to manufacture. On entering Canaan they adopted the agricultural pursuits and the drinking habits of the Canaanites. The Rechabites held out sternly for the good old ways, refusing to build houses, sow the soil, plant vineyards or drink wine (Jer. 35: 1-11). This point is worthy of note because not infrequently in Christian history reformatory movements have been couched in terms of cultural primitivism, a return to some simpler mode of existence. Commonly in our day, however, the cry is from the city to the country, not from the country to the desert.

To sum up: Judaism steers a middle ground between an ascetic religion renouncing wine as evil per se, and a nature religion using wine to produce religious ecstasy. Drunkenness is reproved, moderation is commended. Total abstinence is represented only by rigoristic minorities.

Early Christianity

Christianity inherited this ethic and very largely reproduced its pattern. Jesus was no Nazirite or Rechabite like John the Baptists, for the "Son of Man came eating and drinking," and could be slandered as "a winebibber and a glutton" (Mat. 11:18-19). At the same time Jesus upbraided the drunken stewards (Mat. 24:49) and introduced an ethical rigorism more exacting than that of Judaism in that an offending eye is to be plucked out and an offending hand is to be cut off (Mat. 5:27-29). The Apostle Paul is more explicit because he was confronted with actual drunkenness within the Christian congregations at a very dangerous point, the celebration of the Lord's Supper. Here was the peril that Christianity might degenerate into an orgiastic nature cult (I Cor. 11:21). The Apostle sternly rebuked inebriety. "Let us walk becomingly as in the day, not in revelling and drunkenness" (Rom. 13:12). Among the offenses which exclude from the King of God is drunkenness (I Cor. 6:10). The antidote in the New Testament is not total abstinence, for Timothy may take a little wine for his stomach's sake (I Tim. 5:23), but first the avoidance of evil company. With the drunkard the Christian should not eat (I Cor. 5:11). The real cure is that "ye be not drunken with wine...but filled with the Spirit" (Eph. 5:18). As a rule for conduct Paul formulates a principle of consideration for the weaker brother. "Let no man put a stumbling block in his brother's way...All things indeed are clean...but it is good not to eat flesh, nor to drink wine, nor to do anything whereby thy brother stumbleth" (Rom. 14:13-23).

The ethic of the New Testament was appropriated by the early Church and modified occasionally in the direction of a greater rigorism as a safeguard to Christian morale in the period of persecution. Total abstinence, however, was not enjoined as a general practice. The normal attitude is represented by Clement of Alexandria in a book called The Instructor, in which he inveighs against all excesses and indelicacies in eating and drinking and especially upbraids drunkenness, while recognizing that a moderate use of wine rejoices the heart. Incidentally, in the course of his discussion, he displays a rather broad acquaintance with at least the names of the choicest varieties. At the same time voluntary abstinence is commendable, especially in the young.

Total abstinence was made obligatory in the early Church only by ascetic heretics who, in an age of persecution, readily fell into the error of regarding the material world as evil. Various Gnostics abstained from contact with women, war and wine for the sake of holiness, and in the celebration of the Lord's Supper substituted water for wine. Hence they were nicknamed Aquarians. The same practice prevailed for a time in the orthodox churches of northern Africa where the motive appears to have been not asceticism but the fear that in persecution the Christian would betray himself through the smell of wine on his breath at an unusually early hour of the morning. Bishop Cyprian replied, "Are you ashamed of the blood of Christ?" The sacramental use of wine soon displaced that of water. The danger that actual intoxication might receive a religious sanction was obviated by sublimation into a spiritual intoxication, a **sobria inebrietas,** which runs all through the works of the Greek and Latin fathers to reappear in the great medieval mystic, Bernard of Clairvaux.

The Catholic Ethic

The reconciliation of Christianity with the state made the new religion popular and led to accessions with unseemly haste and all too little preparation. The way was made easier by relaxing the standards. St. Augustine tells us that frequently, when the heathen hesitated to embrace the faith for fear of having to renounce the tippling of pagan festivals, the Church relaxed and countenanced drinking in commemoration of the martyrs. Augustine was doing his best to stamp out the practice in his diocese of northern Africa. St. Basil was similarly outraged by the revelry accompanying the celebration of Easter. But neither enjoined a total abstinence. St. Basil, even in his monastic rule, recommended only self-discipline and variation in practice according to individual need. St. Augustine, writing against a new variety of religious ascetics, the Manichaeans, defended wine as a gift of God.

The rise of monasticism introduced no essential change. The movement was a protest against the corruption of secular and even of ecclesiastical society. To escape contamination the monks fled to the desert. So great was their despair of any Christian society upon earth that they renounced propagation and lived in segregated communities of men and women. In consequence, the quelling of sexual desire became, for a period, a positive obsession, and the means employed was mortification of the flesh by fasting and abstinence. Yet the Rule of St. Benedict did not prohibit wine and the earlier rigor was soon so far relaxed that the Benedictines and the Chartreuses became famous for their vintages.

The Middle Ages offered nothing new in principle, only a constant recurrence of the ancient abuses and the traditional correctives. The holy days of the Church were celebrated with conviviality. There were church-ales, Whitsun ales. What we now call a bridal party was then a bride-ale. The Church inveighed against all such abuses. Occasional drunkenness was branded as a venial sin and habitual drunkenness as a mortal sin. The drunkard was pilloried from the pulpit. All of the burlesques of the English stage and novel have their prototypes in the medieval satires of the pulpit. The drunkard was ridiculed who, seeing two candles and extinguishing one as superfluous, was amazed to find the other disappear as well. More serious was the situation of the inebriate who came home to find four children instead of two. He accused his wife of irregularity and called upon her to demonstrate her innocence by holding a plowshare which he heated red hot in the fireplace. She consented if he would hand it to her, which he did. The preacher assured his auditors that the Virgin would turn away her face from the prayer of a monk whose breath was redolent of wine. The ideal of temperance was at least so well established that satires on clerical intemperance were as funny then as they have been ever since. No more blasphemous piece of buffoonery could be conceived than a parody called <u>The Mass of the Drunkards</u>. The lines of the mass, which read **per Dominum nostrum qui vivit et regnat per saecula saeculorum** (through our Lord who lives and reigns through the ages and ages), were turned into **per dominum nostrum reum Bacchum, qui bibit et poculat per omnia pocula poculorum** (through our lord Bacchus who drinks and guzzles through the cups of the cups). As an example of the same type of literature in modern times we have the skit of Alphonse Daudet concerning Pere Gaucher, who imperils his immortal soul to invent a choicer cordial for the profit of the monastery; or the hilarity of Dickens in the <u>Pickwick Papers</u> over the exploits of the red-nosed Pastor Stiggins at the session of the Brick Lane Branch of the United Grand Junction Ebenezer Temperance Association.

But to return to the earlier centuries. A new possibility was introduced when the Roman Empire gave its patronage to the Church. Christian ideals could then be embodied in secular legislation to be enforced by the state. In other words, the door was open for prohibition. No ruler attempted it in the Christian Roman Empire, nor in the west during the Middle Ages, but regulation of the sale and consumption of liquor by rulers, whether ecclesiastical or secular, was very common during this period. Sumptuary legislation was frequent enough long before the period of the Protestant Reformation.

During the Middle Ages instances of total abstinence are hard to find. The end of that period saw the resurgence of ascetic sects such as the Cathari, resembling the ancient Gnostics. They may have been total abstainers. Bernard of Clairvaux says of them that their faces were pale with fasting. One may perhaps infer that their noses were not red with tippling. But that they were complete abstainers is not clear, since they allowed the use of wine in the sacrament.

Early Protestantism

The Protestant Reformation brought at first no great change in the picture. Martin Luther, when he abolished monasticism and inaugurated that attitude which was to make matrimony almost a prerequisite for a Protestant clergyman, did not compensate by rigorism as to drink. On the contrary, he was somewhat convivial. Once, when at table with his colleagues, he pointed to a stein girt with three rings. The top one, he said, stood for the Ten Commandments, the middle ring for the Apostles' Creed, and the bottom for the Lord's Prayer. Then Luther drained the stein at a draught and refilling it handed it to his friend Agricola who, to Luther's intense amusement, could not get beyond the Ten Commandments. But Luther was no drunkard. Melanchthon testified that he was abstemious and, under the stress of work, would often fast for days. Luther had no use for drunkenness and scathingly denounced his fellow Germans and even his own prince for lapses. Luther's matured attitude is well expressed in his commentary on the miracle at Cana. Jesus turned water into wine. Let us not be scandalized, commented Luther, if some one should take a little more than was necessary for thirst and grow merry, but alas! in our day we drink until we are soused; we are swine, not men.

Not to Luther nor to Lutheranism are we to look for the origin of the modern Protestant campaign against all drink. Nor is the source to be found in the Anglican Church. On this point Lutheranism and Anglicanism are at one with Catholicism. The reason is that they are all churches of the masses, including their membership, whenever possible, all the babies born into the community and baptized into the church. Any church whose membership is not more selective cannot be too rigoristic in ethics.

Another type of Protestantism arose, in the sixteenth century, which insisted that the Church should be a city of the saints no matter how small, and should exclude the unworthy from her membership. The code of conduct demanded of the saints was exacting. This had been the pattern of English and American sectarianism. Its prototype in the Germany of the Reformation was Anabaptism. The movement was not ascetic in the sense of the ancient Gnostics. The Anabaptists did not eschew marriage, and required only moderation in food and drink, but they were ethical rigorists who criticized the Lutheran Reformation for failure to produce a manifest change in moral demeanor. One of the marks of the true Christian is sobriety. The rule of the Hutterian Brethren (1545) forbade any member of the society to be a public innkeeper or to sell wine and beer. The Lutheran Formula of Concord enumerated among the errors of the Anabaptists that a Christian might not keep an inn. A Lutheran minister in 1531 testified that they best way for a suspected Anabaptist to clear himself was to indulge in frequent drinking bouts. These people were ruthlessly suppressed in Germany, and of the of tragedies of the German people is that they have deprived themselves of that sectarian Protestantism which has been such a stimulus to English and American culture.

But the Anabaptists were not without their influence. Their memory afforded an impetus to German Pietism, which, in turn, affected English Methodism. The sectarian Protestantism of Germany likewise made itself felt in the English sectarianism of the seventeenth century among the Quakers. In view of such connections we need feel no surprise to discover the Methodists and the Quakers as the pioneers in the modern temperance crusade.

They were to enlist the support of the churches of Calvinist derivation, and Calvinism itself owes much to its competition with Anabaptism. In order to meet the Anabaptist criticism Calvin adopted a strict discipline. His whole demeanor was more austere than that of the convivial Luther. To be sure, Calvin was not teetotaler. He allowed wine in moderation and did not decline the present of a cask from the town council. At the same time he revived and went beyond the sumptuary legislation of the late Middle Ages. Taverns were suppressed in favor of hostels where food and drink were served only to those who looked as though they would be able to say grace after as well as before partaking, and who agreed to depart from the premises at 9 P.M. Even though the hostels lasted but 3 months, the Genevans were proud of their austerity. A satire, composed by Calvin's colleague Theodore Beza, pictured a Catholic spy coming to Geneva to discover to his amazement how pale were the faces of the heretics. Beza was not slow to point the contrast with the leader of persecution against the Protestants in France, whose nose was the hue of a cardinal's hat. Calvinism contributed to the ultimate temperance campaign a deep moral earnestness, and a readiness, not characteristic of Anabaptism, to make use of the state to institute and enforce a code of conduct. But initial Calvinism was not committed to total abstinence. The modern movement of prohibition is really a combination of the Anabaptist code with the Calvinist program.

But the modern movement did not come until the later eighteenth century. Calvinism was a long time in adopting the Anabaptist code. The Calvinism of Scotland under Knox was no different from that of Geneva under Calvin. Knox had his wine cellar. The Calvinism of English Puritanism exhibited the same general pattern. The Roundheads, indeed, stigmatized the Cavaliers as rowdy and dissolute, but the worse of their offenses appear to have been Sabbath breaking and "God-damn-me oaths," together with pillaging. When King James promulgated a "Book of Lawful Sports" to be played on Sunday afternoons in order to wean the people from "filthy tippling and drunkenness" the Puritans were so outraged by this proposed profanation of the Lord's day that the "Book of Sports" was burned.

New England Puritanism exhibits no marked change. A housewarming had reference to the use of ardent spirits. Even the ordinations of ministers were often unseemly occasions. The shepherd of souls was sore tried to do justice to the hospitality of his flock and get home with the aid only of his crook. Ministers such as the Mathers inveighed against drunkenness. Colonial assemblies regulated the hours of taverns, the quality of beer and the sale to domestics and the Indians, among whom rum wrought havoc. The name Manhattan, by the way, is said to be a corruption of a sentence in the language of the Delawares meaning, "Here we got drunk," referring to their first experience of the hospitality of Hendrik Hudson.

Despite all regulation, excessive drinking continued even among churchmen in New England until the reform movement of the early nineteenth century.

The Temperance Crusade

The initiative in the temperance crusade came from the Methodists and the Quakers, with the Calvinist churches swinging later into line. The Catholics, Lutherans and Episcopalians were reluctant to demand one practice only of their constituents, let alone of society at large. The first temperance reformers were not ascetics fleeing contamination, nor saints aspiring to perfection. Their motivation might rather be called sociological. The evil of drink had grown worse in the eighteenth century due to the displacement of fermented by distilled liquors. A report the His Majesty's Justices of the Peace in 1735-36 lamented the surprising increase of gin-drinking in London in which whole families were involved, parents, children and servants. No one was better acquainted with the prevalent excesses than John Wesley. In the campaign for correction, the alliance of religion with medicine is noteworthy. The inaugurator of the American reform was Benjamin Rush, the Quaker doctor of Philadelphia.

If the program of the reformers became ever more drastic, the reason lay not in any ascetic presuppositions but in the lessons of experience. First came total abstinence from hard liquors, coupled with moderation as to beer and ale. But when it was found that drunkards on the way to reform could lapse as readily on the mild as on the hard, the ban was placed on both, and those who might be able to drink in moderation were urged to refrain entirely our of consideration for the weaker brother. The same moral was deduced from the failure of the Duke of Wellington's attempt to oust hard liquor in Britain through the encouragement of beer. Inebriety was only increased by the Free Beer policy of 1830-69. The failures of regulation likewise drove the temperance movement to the advocacy of prohibition. The course of the movement was very similar in England, Germany and the United States, except that prohibition was achieved only here.

In England the Methodists took the lead. John Wesley, who so well knew the debauchery of the English countryside, lashed out against the sellers of spirituous liquors as poisoners of the people. The Rules of the Society called Methodists, in 1743, required members "to avoid buying or selling spirituous liquors, or drinking them, unless in cases of extreme necessity."

In the United States the Quakers were the most notable exponents of reform. The reputed father of the temperance movement in this country was the Philadelphia doctor, Benjamin Rush. Having observed all too well the evils of excessive drinking in the Revolutionary Army he published a tract entitled An Inquiry into the Effects of Ardent Spirits (1785). His objection was only to the use of distilled liquors. As a substitute he recommended first water, and if that did not suffice, then cider or light wine. Much medical observation was introduced. He closed with a ringing plea to all the churches to join in the crusade. In the following 6 decades his tract circulated 200,000 copies. Another notable Quaker pioneer was Neal Dow, one of the fathers of American prohibition. He was a citizen of Maine. His first enunciation of the principle of prohibition was in 1839. He lived to see it embodied in the law of his state in 1851. Thereafter the cry of the temperance reformers was, "Remember the Maine Liquor Law."

Among the churches of the Calvinist tradition which rallied to the support of the Methodists and the Friends come first the Congregationalists, who were the leaders of the movement in New England from 1810 until the formation of the Temperance Society in 1826. The year 1810 was marked by the indignation of Lyman Beecher when, at his ordination, the sideboard was loaded with decanters containing every liquor in vogue. The talk was jocose and convivial. This said he, "woke me up for the war." He was ardently seconded by Leonard Bacon who, in New Haven in 1829, preached his sermon on "Total Abstinence from Ardent Spirits." By ardent spirits he meant distilled liquors. Beer and wine were not discussed.

With regard to other churches of the Calvinist tradition we may note that the Presbyterians in 1827-30 took a strong stand for total abstinence, and in 1854 endorsed prohibition. The pronouncements of the Baptists were the most rigoristic. The New Jersey Association in 1835 declared that "It is morally wrong in all, and especially in a professor of religion, to manufacture, vend or use such liquors [alcoholic, whether distilled or fermented] as a common article of luxury or living."

The churches with the more inclusive membership, the Catholic, Lutheran and Episcopalian, have been less disposed to general requirements binding upon all members, although of course perfectly ready to bless total abstinence movements within their folds. The approval given by Pope Leo XIII to the Catholic abstinents was similar to a papal sanction of a vow of celibacy or poverty, which is commendable in those who take it, but not required of all. The zeal and effectiveness of thousands of Catholics who did espouse the cause are by no means to be minimized. One thinks of the Confraternity of the Sacred Thirst, and the vigorous support of Cardinal Gibbons and Bishop Ireland who declared that, "to Irishmen particularly, because of their comparative native powerlessness to resist alcohol...I will never cease pointing

THE CONTRIBUTION OF THE MINISTER TO THE TREATMENT OF THE ALCOHOLIC

Otis R. Rice

Rice gives an excellent summary of the special resources and how they can be used to help alcoholics receive appropriate treatment. Originally published in 1951, the advice is still relevant today.

Problems arising from alcohol addiction are encountered by most clergy men in the exercise of their pastoral ministry. The contact may be directly with the alcoholic, or more remotely through the family or associates of the inebriate, in connection with community agencies, or in relations to groups or organizations within the pastor's own parish.

In the past the clergy have generally been no more successful in meeting the difficulties of individual problem drinkers than have physicians or representatives of the law. Indeed, it must be frankly admitted that ministers have often failed because of attitudes or ignorances frequently found among members of their profession.

Currently, however, many pastors are achieving a new understanding of the problem and a fresh recognition of their own unique resources and limitations in dealing with it. This paper will be concerned with a brief survey of the positive and negative adjuncts of the ministry in assisting alcoholics, and with the various areas in which the minister can be related to the prevention and cure of alcohol addiction.

Resources and Limitations

The resources in the gift of the average minister are

those available to him as he attempts any serious problem of pastoral guidance or counseling. His privileged relationship with his people, often built up over years of faithful work, provides for some inebriates or their associates an easy and trusted access to his counsel. In terms of pastoral counseling the "rapport" has often already been established. Previous preaching, teaching or pastoral association has indicated the minister's willingness and availability for helping his parishioners in trouble. He may already possess many insights into individuals and family situations, as a result of earlier pastoral visits or ministrations, which will stand him in good stead as he seeks to understand the factors that have contributed to the present predicament of his parishioner. The authority of office conferred by his ordination may give him a favored position in the eyes of many of his flock, or others outside it, as they contemplate seeking aid. There are those who would more freely seek help from a clergyman than from a physician, psychiatrist, or social worker. He is, in one sense, not a "professional" and this fact may recommend him to some.

Within the framework of organized religion are other resources that have proved valuable in the pastoral guidance of alcoholics. The sense of fellowship or "belongingness" of the worship and social life of the church is one. The frank recognition of the fact of sin and the hope of forgiveness mean much in relation to the guilt so often experienced by the alcoholic. A sound and usable theology helps a man orient toward himself, his fellowmen, and the rest of the world around him. He is given thereby a workable philosophy of life. It provides him with answers or interpretations for some of the most perplexing and soul-shaking experiences out of which alcoholic behavior patterns may arise: loneliness, guilt, failure, success, suffering, sudden responsibility, injustice, inadequacy and hostility. Basically important to the alcoholic is the sense of the existence of God which some ministers are able to instill. If the sufferer can believe that God exists and that He cares greatly for individuals and needs them all for His purposes, a new orientation is often made. Private and corporate prayer, a sense of mission and closeness to God, the sacraments and rites of a religious body, are factors that, under right guidance, can be used by the individual creatively.

The social and activity groups to be found in connection with most churches offer various outlets and experiences which are also helpful in individual rehabilitation.

Although the minister possesses these valuable resources he is nevertheless handicapped by his limitations. In the minds of many he is branded as having a "holier than thou" attitude or as possessing so little knowledge of human problems or human foibles that he would be shocked or incensed or helpless when they are presented. Some pastors are hopelessly sentimental in their sympathy. Others are so unfree emotionally as regards the problem of alcohol that their censoriousness repels and destroys confidence.

Many preachers are so involved with the preparation of sermons or the administrative work of their church that they simply refuse to devote the time and study necessary for the understanding and counseling of alcoholics. Fear of condemnation on the part of an unenlightened congregation for activities on behalf of inebriates deters talks and the dangerous urging of the signing of pledges may handicap others. And there is positive danger in the giving of advice or counsel without adequate study or experience in the field of personal counseling.

Despite a recognition of these real dangers and limitations one believes that opportunities for the well-oriented and trained clergyman are too great to be ignored.

Areas of Contribution

There are several ways in which the minister of religion can assist in the problem of the alcoholic. Briefly to be considered are these:

1. The process of emotional education and the dissemination of the true data regarding alcohol addiction and its treatment.

2. Interpretation of alcohol addiction to families and associates of the alcoholic and guidance in their search for treatment or assistance.

3. Preparation of the alcoholic for accepting treatment and his referral to competent agencies.

4. Actual counseling of the individual alcoholic or groups of alcoholics.

Educational Opportunities

The minister as an educator is in a strong position to influence individual and community attitudes. Preaching, informal congregational instruction, study groups, men's societies, young-people's organizations, teacher-training classes, are some of his opportunities. The formal program of religious education in the church school offers a valuable medium for instruction in the field.

In the past many preachers have inveighed against the evils of drink and have crusaded for temperance. But their information regarding alcohol and its misuse was often fragmentary, distorted, or erroneous. With deeper understanding of the problem and with more scientific knowledge the pastor can give intelligent instruction in a dozen different areas within his parish and community. In a very real sense his work can be preventive. Particularly is this true of his opportunities for long-range emotional education through kindergarten, church school, teacher-training program, and parent study groups. Since religion and emotional life are inextricably related and since the sound, well-adjusted emotional life of the individual is the most certain assurance of freedom from addiction, the importance of the pastor's preventive role is evident.

Moreover, in the normal routine of pastoral care--house-to-house visiting, premarital counseling, administration of the sacraments and rites, personal counseling--there is ample scope for the giving of factual information and the developing of attitudes in individuals and families which will greatly facilitate treatment if alcohol addiction becomes a problem.

Interpretation and Guidance

To the family or associates of the problem drinker the intelligent pastor can offer valuable assistance. His attitude, understanding and factual knowledge can be constructive factors in the situation. When the pastor shows that he is neither making judgments nor offering maudlin sympathy but faces the difficulty as a problem to be solved, and not alone as a sin to be punished or a tragedy to be prayerfully deplored, others who respect him will alter their attitudes to conform to his own. As the pastor shows, without undue display of emotion, that he understands both the predicament of the alcoholic and also that of his relatives or colleagues, his influence and authority increase and his guidance and counsel are sought. In some instances he may be the only one concerned who knows the most recent facts regarding the causes, treatment and prognosis of alcohol addiction.

When the pastor, though his attitude, knowledge of the facts, and his experience with alcoholics, is able to persuade the family or colleagues of the alcoholic to look at the situation more objectively, many tensions with respect to the inebriate are relieved. Indeed, such a change in attitude toward him may in itself be the evocative factor in his decision to seek treatment or even in the final cure.

A valuable aid to the pastor is suitable literature regarding inebriety that may be placed in the hands of families and sometimes of the alcoholic as well. It is obvious that the minister's familiarity with the local resources--psychiatrists, social agencies, clinics and Alcoholics Anonymous groups--will help him in his relations with concerned.

Preparation for Treatment and Referral

A vitally important function of the clergy is the preparation of parishioners for referral to other agencies for professional assistance which the minister is unable or unprepared to give. To win the confidence of one in difficulty, to counsel him to the acceptance of treatment, is one of the most delicate and productive phases of pastoral care.

For many pastors this will be the most important part that can be played in the treatment of the alcoholic. Moreover, in this connection the intelligent cooperation of the minister with the agency to which referral is made can become productive. For during treatment a religious ministry to the patient can be extremely helpful. But both the clergyman and the other agency must understand their particular phases of work. Doubtless it will be possible for the pastor to provide material for the case record, form his own pastoral observations, which will be valuable in the therapeutic process, but this must be done with due regard to the confidences of the patient and the privileged nature of the minister's relationship.

Pastoral Counseling

The only phase of the minister's work with alcoholics that can be considered as "treatment" is pastoral counseling. In recent years this approach has been studied and tried by an increasing number of civilian ministers and service chaplains. The hit-or-miss giving of advice, indiscriminate use of prayer or "doing good for others," has been replaced by a careful attempt to understand the individual problems of parishioners and to encourage the use, by the individual, of the resources--religious, social and personal--to be found in his situation. One definition of pastoral counseling might be cited to indicate the trend in attitude:

Pastoral counseling is adept listening whose aim is to discover the internal tensions and external pressures with which the parishioner is struggling; to evaluate his capacity for dealing with these tensions and pressures. Then without removing his personal responsibility, to marshal his capacities and resources (personal, religious and social), so as to relieve these pressures to a point where he, with an understanding of his situation, is able to deal with them himself.

There is now a considerable body of literature in the field of pastoral counseling. Carefully taken case records of successes and failures in pastoral counseling have been studied. Although the results of the work have been modest, there is good reason to believe that this disciplined, understanding approach to individual problems by the clergy will be fruitful. In relation to the rehabilitation of alcoholics one must not be too sanguine. The alcoholic presents deep-seated and complex emotional, physical and social problems. In many instances pastoral counseling may not prove effective. But in many others the minister's use of this technique can be definitely helpful. While there are no statistical data available, it can be said that those clergy who have studied the field carefully and who have received training are able to report encouraging results.

Pastoral counseling requires of the minister (in addition to his training) a large proportion of his available time, great patience, and considerable intuitive skill in understanding the varied mechanisms of personality encountered in such intimate work with individuals. It means also the routine of numerous conferences, careful recording and study of case records, great restraint in the giving of advice, and the disciplined use of such religious resources as prayer, corporate worship, sacraments and rites.

But the trained minister is in a favored position in dealing with such factors as grief, guilt, hostility and the sense of inadequacy which so often underlie the conflicts of the alcoholic. Within his own parish or community are many educational, vocational, medical and social resources which can become adjuncts of this counseling when used with care and discrimination. And, as has already been said, the minister, through his previous pastoral ministrations, contacts and preaching, may have gained insights into the individual or his family and may have paved the way to a confidential relationship in which much can be accomplished.

The Minister and the Alcoholic

In this paper the minister's contribution to the problems of the alcoholic has been somewhat sketchily divided into the educational opportunity, the relation to family or associates, preparation and referral of the alcoholic for treatment, and the pastoral counseling of alcoholics. Most ministers can safely and, I believe, productively undertake the first three approaches. Study of the facts relating to alcohol addiction must be made. Objectivity and perspective must be maintained. Disappointments, sacrifice of time, misunderstandings, must be faced. But to the extent suggested, clergymen can make a contribution toward the rehabilitation of alcoholics.

Only a few ministers are qualified for or should rightfully undertake the professional counseling of alcoholics. But those few who, with full knowledge of their limitations, are willing to equip themselves for the work will do much toward the cure of the alcoholic and the better understanding of those factors that make this distressing situation possible.

Training

Ministers who seek training in pastoral counseling of the alcoholic will find as yet no specialized academic course offered them. [Although true in 1951, this statement is no longer true.] Instruction in mental hygiene, psychology, guidance and counseling is offered in several good universities. Courses are given in the field of pastoral psychology in some theological seminaries. Seminars and conferences on pastoral counseling are conducted for ministers by national religious organizations. More specialized clinical training for seminarians and clergy is given by several foundations. The summer session of the Section on Alcohol Studies at Yale provides various opportunities for learning the facts about alcohol and alcohol addiction.

The pastor who wishes to do pastoral counseling in the field certainly needs a wide background of reading in the psychology of personality, mental hygiene, counseling, and the scientific facts regarding alcohol. But beyond this he needs training and guidance through seminars, a clinical training program, or experience of being himself counseled by an expert, before he can very humbly undertake his difficult but rewarding task.

This article originally appeared in Pastoral Psychology *2.13 (1951): 250-256. It is reprinted with permission.*

For Further Reading on
Historical Issues and Alcoholics Anonymous

(1976). Alcoholics Anonymous. New York, New York: Alcoholics Anonymous World Services, Inc.

This book is the basic text of AA. It explains the program. Stories of recovered alcoholics are included.

Bishop, C., & Pittman, B. (1989). The Annotated Bibliography of Alcoholics Anonymous: 1939 - 1989. Wheeling, West Virginia: The Bishop of Books.

Bishop and Pittman list and annotate over 1,400 books, articles, pamphlets, and brochures which deal with AA Seventy-five percent of the articles are annotated. The book is a wealth ofinformation.

Conley, P. C., & Sorensen, A. A. (1971). The Staggering Steeple: The Story of Alcoholism and the Churches. Philadelphia: Pilgrim Press.

The book explores the church's social and cultural attitudes toward alcoholism in American society.

Courtwright, D., Joseph, H., & Des Jarlais, D. (1989). Addicts Who Survived: An Oral History of Narcotic Use In America, 1923- 1965. Knoxville, Tennessee: University of Tennessee Press.

The authors focus on the lives of middle and upper class addicts. An historical essay serves as the book's introduction.

(1980). Dr. Bob and the Good Oldtimers: A Biography, With Recollections of Early AA in the Midwest. New York, New York: Alcoholics Anonymous World Services, Inc.

This book is the official biography of Bob Smith, one of AA's co-founders.

Hunter, W. (1988). AA's Roots in the Oxford Group. New York: Alcoholics Anonymous.

Hunter provides a good, basic summary of AA's debt to the Oxford Group. Contributions made by Samuel Shoemaker, Ebby T., and Carl Jung are explained.

Jellinek, E. M. (1960). The Disease Concept of Alcoholism. New Haven, Connecticut: College and University Press.

Although the disease concept of alcoholism had its roots in the eighteenth century, this book was the first contemporary book to promote this theory.

Kurtz, E. (1979). Not God: A History of Alcoholics Anonymous. Center City, MN: Hazelden.

In this history of Alcoholics Anonymous, Kurtz focusses on the fact that AA teaches alcoholics that they are "not God." After giving the history of AA, he provides an interpretation of AA spirituality in the larger context of American social and religious history.

Kurtz, E., & Kurtz, L. F. (Winter, 1985). The Social Thought of Alcoholics. Journal of Drug Issues, 119-134.

The authors trace the historic roots of theological attitudes held toward alcohol in America. Two paradigms are offered as to how alcoholism might be viewed: the religious, or postmodern, and the modern disease concept.

Lender, M., & Martin, J. K. (1982). Drinking in America: A History. New York: Free Press.

Lender and Martin trace the history of drinking in America by giving special attention to religious/moral attitudes toward alcohol and alcohol use.

(1979). Lois Remembers: Memoirs of the Co-founder of Al-Anon and Wife of the Co-founder of Alcoholics Anonymous. New York, New York: Al-Anon Family Group Headquarters, Inc.

This is the autobiography of Lois Wilson, founder of Al-Anon.

Maxwell, M. A. (1984). The AA Experience: A Close-up View for Professionals. New York, New York: McGraw-Hill Book Company.

Maxwell gives an introduction to the AA program. Not an alcoholic himself, Maxwell began his research in 1949 and became a noted authority on the program.

McCarthy, K. (1984). Early Alcoholism Treatment: The Emmanuel Movement and Richard Peabody. Journal of Studies on Alcohol, 45(1), 59-74.

McCarthy gives a history of the Emmanuel Movement and of the work of Richard Peabody.

(1984). Pass It On: The Story of Bill Wilson and How the AA Message Reached the World. New York, New York: Alcoholics Anonymous World Services, Inc.

This book is the official biography of Bill Wilson, one of AA's co-founders.

Pittman, B. (1988). AA: The Way It Began. Seattle: Glen Abby.

Before giving the early history of AA, Pittman explains alcoholism treatments of the 1890s. He also gives information about prohibition, the Oxford Group, and the life of Bill Wilson.

Robertson, N. (1988). Getting Better: Inside Alcoholics Anonymous. New York: William Morrow.

Robertson, a member of AA, gives her view of AA history. This book was controversial when it was published because Robertson broke her anonymity. However, it does give a good overview of the AA program.

Stoil, M. (1987). Salvation and Sobriety. Alcohol Health and Research World, 11(3), 14-17.

Stoil gives an historical overview of the Salvation Army's work with alcoholics in the United States.

Warren C. (1970). Thirty-One Years in Cleveland AA. NCCA Blue Book, 22, 132-144.

Warren tells of his addiction to alcohol and recovery through AA.

Whealon, J. F. (1976). The Churches Reply to the Alcoholic Plea. NCCA Blue Book, 28, 1-7.

Archbishop Whealon gives an overview of the church's response to alcoholism from the colonial period to present.

William W. (1949). The Society of Alcoholics Anonymous. American Journal of Psychiatry, 106(5), 370-375.

The co-founder of AA uses his own story of addiction and recovery as the basis from which to describe the AA program.

STORIES OF RECOVERY

PREACHING WE DON'T NEED:
A PRIEST'S STORY

Alcoholics, whether they are priests or not, do not need preaching. What they need is active participation in AA In sharing his story, this anonymous priest explains why.

Some years ago, a middle-aged priest slowly came to in a large hospital. A psychiatrist, a physician, and the chaplain were trying to talk quietly to him. But the priest's mind seemed very cobwebby, and he just couldn't understand the words spoken. Five days later, he shakily went home. This was the fourth time the alcoholic minister of God had been found unconscious from taking alcohol and pills. On another occasion, two alert policemen had kept him from leaping off a high bridge in drunken despair. Sanitariums, several psychiatrists, and the loss of five positions had not been enough to halt his destructive drinking. But this time he fell to his knees, finally admitted that he was totally powerless over the bottle, and cried out, "Oh dear God, please **help** me!" He then fell confidently and tranquilly asleep.

A local priest who was a member of AA came to his room the very next morning, encouraged him in warm and empathetic words, and took him to an AA meeting that night. Instantly, the discouraged priest knew that he "belonged here." So far, he has not returned to alcohol, thanks to his Higher Power. He is emotionally sober and happy. The very university that once fired him has received him back, and he is totally involved in counseling other alcoholics and their families.

I am that priest. For several years now, in the course of counseling and directing serenity retreats for alcoholics and their spouses, I have continually reflected on the reasons for

AA's effectiveness. In all humility, we are entitled to observe that it has saved hundreds of thousands of human lives, as well as preventing millions of dollars of loss to industry and government.

First, to my mind AA works so well because it is directed straight at one particular problem **alone:** how to attain and retain sobriety. This concentrated approach seems to work better, for most alcoholics, than the rather general approach of organized religions. Even the tenets of my own Christian faith and the exercise of a priestly ministry did not keep me from excessive drinking, but the head-on spiritual philosophy of the Twelve Steps finally worked when all else had failed. Although it is true that some have called AA "a natural religion," they will readily admit that it is not sectarian and will fit any creed, Christian or otherwise. Nor does it hurt AA in any way that many members choose to return to a definite religious faith as they mature, making the free choice of a more formal worship of God.

In my own case, withdrawal from alcohol left a large vacuum within my spirit. This had to be filled by something. Some of the alcoholics I counsel relapse because they refuse to fill their lonely emptiness with a positive substitute. The early members of AA bequeathed us a spiritual and positive program that can fill our yearning souls with reciprocal love for God and service to our alcoholic neighbors. What **more** can an empty-hearted alcoholic ask for?

AA works well for me because it demands of me an **unconditional reliance** on the very real power of my unseen Higher Power, who I call God. Starting with the humble admission of the First Step, we rise through the newfound hope and faith of the Second Step to the total commitment of the Third Step. The Diving Physician accepts my total surrender of will and life to His providence. From this moment, everything seems to go better for me spiritually and socially, despite the fresh problems that arise, as they do for all of us. During the past thirty-five years, countless physicians and psychiatrists have been amazed at the effectiveness of AA's simple program. To these helpful professional men, members like me can only say, "AA works because God works!"

AA also has helped to restructure my whole personality toward what God intended me to be. Although some professionals today are inclined to agree with Dr. E. M. Jellinek's 1945 remark in Dallas that "Any normal person can become an alcoholic," it remains true that all of us were temporarily unbalanced by alcohol. Through the Fourth, Fifth, and Tenth Steps, I have learned to substitute new, positive, and healthy emotions for harmful ones. Through the AA program, all of us can begin to achieve a new awareness of our own uniqueness and God-given individuality.

AA works because it offers warm fellowship, as I immediately discovered. Within it, I found the social strength of a sympathetic group, dedicated to a new way of involved living. Interesting and dependable friends began to show surprising concern for me. And I said to myself, "They have all been through it, too; they know." Despite our human faults, our Fellowship simply isn't like the competitive world around us, where you often wonder who will try to cut your throat next. In AA, we can again relate well to people and be socially comfortable. No wonder the first woman alcoholic to enter AA exclaimed, "Now I am no longer alone!"

AA works because it includes the magic-working "therapy" of friendly group discussions. For me, they have certainly proven to be the most effective way of staying sober, provided only that they are united with the spiritual activity of the Twelve Steps. Several outside groups that I lead in discussing basic qualities of human maturity follow the line of AA discussions, and even utilize helpful thoughts from co-founder Bill W.'s writings. In the experiences, problems, and solutions of members who speak at AA meetings, I see myself mirrored more clearly. Then I understand what I must do to live a richer spiritual life.

All of us realize that doing Twelfth Step work is a key reason for the continuing sobriety so many have found through AA. To develop this would require much space, and Bill W. has already done it for us. My **personal** practice of the Twelve Steps is greatly helped when, in my individual and group counseling, I am able to assist other sufferers into the programs of both AA and Al-Anon. My small role here ends when I have found sponsors for them, but the warm feeling of accomplishment under God always remains.

Finally, to me the principal reason for the effectiveness of AA seems to be the mysterious power of simple prayer, so well outlined in the Eleventh Step. Bill W. was certainly right when he once wrote that the Eleventh Step "can keep us growing." Surely, all of our personal gifts and spiritual progress must come to us from our Higher Power. Where else? It is unfortunate that, in a few groups of AA, there is a soft-pedaling of God and the spiritual. Preaching we don't need, but prayer we do! The most interesting meeting I attended last year was one devoted entirely to various ways of praying well. "More things are wrought by prayer than this world dream of" is a statement always borne out in simple practice, at least in my own ministerial life.

Like our wise co-founder Bill W., I have grown to be grateful that I experienced the leveling pains of alcoholism. How very true it is that membership in AA is a great privilege, carrying with it a deep responsibility to others who we shall help. The way in which I express my sincere gratitude every night is to say humbly, "Thank you, dear God, thank you for Alcoholics Anonymous."

ME LLAMO ROBERTO Y SOY ALCOHOLICO

Roberto S.

If Roberto walked into your office, would you have the resources to help him? Most people who read Alcoholism and the Parish Priest will have difficulty understanding Roberto's message because of the language barrier. Yet many alcoholics find themselves closed off from alcohol services because Spanish is their primary language.

Me llamo Roberto y soy alcohólico: Nunca crei que hiba a decir eso. . . menos en público. . .

Soy Mexicano/Americano; el septimo de 10 hijos, de padres mexicanos, oriundo del Estado de Michigan. Era una familia muy tradicional, con todas las costumbres de una familia mexicana. Mi padre tenia un billar, y ahi fúe donde formé muchos de mis valores y ideas, valores que hiba a sequir por los proximos 30 años, y siempre con el pensamiento que era . . . "normal" . . .

Empezé a tomar vino a los 14 años en un baile que habia organizado mi padre. Los clientes del billar me daban pruebas de sus botellas de coca-cola, era mi iniciacion a ser muy macho, muy hombre, muy adulto; despertaba con un dolor de cabeza el dia siguiente. Mi Mamá no me habló por tres dias y si hablaba era para reganarme: "No sabes decir no? Te forsaron tomar esas bebidas?" me preguntaba mi Mamá. "Si van a un lago y se tiran clavados y se ahogan . . . Tu vas hacer lo mismo?" Me volvio ella a preguntar, mientras mi padre decia, "Ya, ya, ya, asi aprendera a hacerse hombre, ya no lo va hacer y lo segui haciendo, durante 30 años; . . .Mis valores consistian: cuando estas tomado, te diviertas, te sientes mejor, te relajas, hasta bailes mejor y puedes echar los gritos con mas ganas, y los amigos te respetan por la cantidad de alcohol que consumes.

A los 18 años, ingresé al servicio militar, no a proteger a mi pais si no a mejorar la cantidad de alcohol que consumia. En la fiesta navidena de 1957, sali a celebrar año nuevo con un amigo y desperté en la cárcel, que pena le causé a mis padres, el Juez me ordenó pagar una multa de 5.00dlls. y que regresara a mi estacion militar. Mi padre y un hermano, fueron a recojerme y pagar mi multa. Regresamos a casa para me despedida, un desayuno mexicano, huevos con chorizo, frijoles, salsa. Y mi madre comentaba, "Ah hijo! mio, cuando vas a aprender a decir no?"

Regresé después de 4 años y consegui trabajo de cartero. Comenzé a mis padres a regalar cosas que el queria, ya que yo miraba que con su trabajo no lo podia obtener. Primero arreglamos la casa por afuera despues diferentes cosas como muebles, máquinas de lavar ropa, secadora, etc.

En este tiempo fué cuando conoci a mis primos en Mexico para ser mas exacto de Piedras Negras Coahuila' aprendiendo de ellos una palabra nueva que se llama "cruda."

Y asi siguio mi vida sin meta alguna y cada fin de semana "crudo" y yo muy macho y muy hombre, por los regalos que le daba a mis padres. . .Muy buen hijo. . . .

Las crudas siguieron y fui a la cárcel tres veces en los 60's, no me importaba nada y nadie me podia decir nada, era el hijo bueno. . .Mi padre siempre me decia, si tienes algún problema platicamelo y yo los arreglo. . . .yo no me he muerto, siempre te he ayudar. . .y yo, no lo cría. . .No me acuerdo mucho de la enfermedad que tubo mi padre del cozón. Pero en Abril de '65, y yo con una cruda tremenda, acostado en el sofá viendo t.v. Mi hermano llevó a mi madre a la tienda, "Cuida a tu papá ahorita vengo..." De regreso hayó a mi padre muerto en su cama! Y yo -- ni cuenta medí. Porque no habia aprendido a decir no!

Mi papá era poeta y para mis compleaños de 1962, me escribio lo siguiente:

No temas que la gente algun dia
Te critiquen por borracho y parrandero
Diles que eres hijo de Sofia,
Y de Trino, el poeta aventurero.

Y asi traté de sequir mi vida, como papá lo habia descrito. . .Los amigos de México, me habian puesto de sobre nombre "el General," porque aguantaba, una botella de tequila sauza lo cambiaron a chorcholotas!

En el '75, tuve un infarto, y el doctor me prohibio el alcohol. No tomé por dos años, los cuale fueron los mejores que desempeñen mi trabajo del correo. En el '78, regresé a San Luis Potosi México y en una reunión me invitaron a tomar una copa, a salúd de un gran amigo que habia fallecido. . .No gracias. "Un Mexicano no se raja!" dijeron y empezé a tomar nuevamente. En el'81, tuve otro infarto! Mi última cruda fué en Julio del '80 gracias a Dios fui a mi primer junta de A.A. Los resos de mi madre fueron contestados. . .

Hay una canción que dice: "La vida no vale nada" pero es un error. La vida si vale! y desde entonces me dedico a ensenar como decir no!

The passage from "En El Dia de tu Santo--A Lorenzo" reprinted with permission from Poesias (Vol. 2) by Trinidad V. Sanchez, Jr., S.J. (Lansing, MI: El Renacimiento Renaissance Publications, 1985).

SHATTERED!

AA does not promise that recovered alcoholics will never face crisis. It promises that crisis can be faced without drinking. When this anonymous author discovered he had AIDS, his world was shattered, but he remained sober.

My increased reliance upon alcohol over my years of drinking gradually consumed my feelings of self-worth. The more I tried to regain the self-worth that was slipping from me, the more I drank. The more I drank, the more unsure of myself I became.

My alcohol use became alcohol abuse as I became increasingly frustrated with my life and my surroundings. Gradually I saw no way out. Drinking had become a two-edged sword; it cut into me while it was protecting me. Then I came to the solution. I didn't have to drink.

I realized during recovery, and attendance at AA meetings, that my feelings of self-worth did not depend upon popularity or other external measures of acceptance. Self-worth became self-perception. I learned from Chapter Five that I was not a saint. I learned from my sponsor that I was not a devil, either.

I learned to be responsible for my actions and conduct, and to give others the right to their opinions. During the slow redevelopment of my self-worth, I realized that my feelings as an adolescent were different from my feelings as an adult. My values were different. As long as I held onto the self-worth of my immature self, I would never mature and would never experience what I later came to realize was essential to my emotional recovery: "To thine own self be true."

Self-worth began to develop slowly, then accelerated as I began to work with those experiencing the same inferior feelings I had felt. I became dependent upon strengths other than alcohol, became free of the bondage of self, and finally became respected by people I had helped.

Then the accumulated years of self-worth were shattered. Just before my AA anniversary I was hospitalized for a pneumonia which did not respond to standard treatment. A lung biopsy was ordered. As I was wheeled gasping into the procedure, I kept thinking, "Thy will not mine be done."

The doctor who performed the procedure was with me when I woke from the sedatives. In my still drugged head I heard him say, "Your lung biopsy showed pneumocystis carini pneumonia, a secondary condition of Acquired Immune Deficiency Syndrome. I am sorry."

My self-worth was leaving as he said these words. I felt like a worthless leper. My worth plunged over the next few weeks when I was dismissed from my job, consumed years of savings, then sold off valued art and furnishings to meet expenses. My "significant other" left during a panic attack and did not return. I felt alone, powerless, and out of control. I was reaching another bottom.

I had been around AA long enough to know that when we reach a crisis we can neither postpone nor evade; that we realize God is everything, or He is nothing. I knew the most important thing in my life was the maintenance of my recovery and that heavily intertwined within that recovery was my self-worth. I knew I was headed for trouble.

After I made my funeral arrangements I talked to a close non-AA friend. I told him how final everything felt, and that I had returned to smoking tobacco. His reply was, "Why don't you go ahead and have a couple of drinks to take the edge off? You're not going to live long anyway."

God works in strange ways through different people. I felt the power of an anger I hadn't felt in years. Then a thought crossed my mind that crowded out all else: "I had to work too hard to get where I am today to let anything take it away from me." Then came the second, more gentle thought: "Will you let another illness take away your recovery?" I realized that God was doing for me what I could not do for myself. He was giving me direction.

I had developed my self-worth by sharing my experience, strength, and hope with others. I reaffirmed that my life was in divine order and prayed for the strength to experience rejection if that was his will for me. Then I went to one of my larger home meetings, took the floor, and let the members know what had happened to my health. Some were unconcerned, some took to gossip, others tearfully thanked me for what I had quietly done for them over the years. I did not experience public rejection, and for that I am grateful.

Some of my health has returned, and I have resumed the AA service work to which I am accustomed. This service has given me a feeling of purpose. My self-worth has improved. Although my life will never again be the same, I am grateful for the training we receive to cope with crisis. AA has given me a purpose and a continued chance with my recovery.

AN END TO AN ENDLESS STRUGGLE

Spanky

Spanky took AA's second and third steps while in prison. In this story, he tells about how he came to believe in a power greater than himself and how he turned his will and life over to the care of his higher power.

For years I have fought the idea of religion of God, and of a Higher Power. I was born and raised Catholic. I went to Catholic Church for my first years of school. I resented the fact that I was forced to memorize the prayers or face the yardstick over my knuckles. When I asked where God was, they said, "UP THERE." I looked up and didn't see nothing that I haven't seen before. "UP WHERE?" Why can't I see him?

I was told God didn't like bad kids and that I would go to hell for my sins. I was told of his Ten Commandments that he gave us for his laws. I don't believe there is one that I haven't broken. Once I realized this with the thought that I was going to hell. I gained an attitude that seeing I'm going anyway, I may as well go all the way.

I felt that if a Higher Power or God would damn me for messing up, I wanted no part of it at all. I became an Atheist - A non believer - or whatever you want to term it as. I tried to be my own God. I tried to run things my way. I wanted people and things to be my way. I could do anything that I was of mind to. But I couldn't do anything. I made up my own God in the form of sniffing glue, smoking pot, taking acid and drinking. Anything that made me feel okay was my Higher Power, mainly because I couldn't make me feel better. I had to use whatever. I became a garbage head, using absolutely anything to feel better. And way down deep inside, to hide from that childhood version of a God that was out to get me for my wrongs in life.

After I stopped using substances to make me feel better, I was faced with this God thing again. I want to stay straight, but this God and Higher Power scare me. I mean really scare me. They wanted me to turn my will over to the care of God or a Higher Power? For what execution? A sentence to Hell? I hid from him so long, now they wanted me to face Him! We're talking serious fear here.

People offered me their God, but I wanted my very own. Why get one that someone else had?

Then I would still argue the point of this religious stuff. I would rebel from reflex.

Then someone asked me, "What would you want your Higher Power to be?" And after thinking hard about this, I decided I wanted a forgiving and understanding Higher Power. Someone to be there for me. Someone to accept me for me. Someone that would not damn me and send me to that "Hell." Someone that can handle things for me because I can't handle them no more. I tried and failed. Someone to give me a chance. Then this person says to me, "Suppose you had a Higher Power all along that was waiting for you to get tired of doing his job, so he let you see for yourself that it was a hard one. And suppose that if you gave Him a chance now that He would take over if you let Him. And that with His help things would get better."

It gave me something to think about and think about. I thought back to the times of attempting suicide, accidents I got into and all the times of driving under the influence. I didn't die or get killed. Was I being given a chance then? Something. It was surely something. Then the one thing that really stuck in my head was the "Footprints" that I read. It really made me think of how I got through the lowest points in my life. I guess I wasn't really alone.

Today I will say that my Higher Power is forgiving, loving and understanding. He is strong to be able to carry my weight and only want me to be willing to let him in return. That is the best deal I made in my whole life.

He will take over and manage my life and all I have to do is let him.

I am not no born again Christian, I am not a Bible beater and I'm not talking religion.

I'm talking of a Higher Power. Something greater than myself. A friend that I can talk to anytime and about anything. And a friend is something I can believe in. You can believe a Higher Power to be anything, just don't think it's you. It won't work.

I think this is my start to the third step. Maybe an end to an endless struggle. I have to give it a chance, I've tried everything else.

This article originally appeared in Hilltop View AA Group *(1988), a booklet produced at the Connecticut Correctional Institution at Enfield. It is reprinted with permission from the author.*

GAY ALCOHOLIC PRIEST

Father Bob

*It is often said that "we are as sick as
our secrets." Honesty is often difficult,
but it is crucial to full recovery. Father
Bob's story demonstrates this point.*

My ordination as a priest of the Roman Catholic Church
was a red-letter day for me. It freed me from stifling
seminary-control to liberating self-control. One significant
sign of this new life was freedom to drink alcohol without
fear of harsh punishment.

My reputation in the parish quickly spread as a heavy
drinker who appreciated good scotch. Gift-giving occasions
such as Christmas and birthday should have signaled that I
was drinking too much--most friends thought of me in
relation to alcohol and remembered the occasion with a
fifth.

Without seeing a connection, my health deteriorated as
my drinking increased. I experienced sharp pains in the
stomach, I was always tired, my vision was blurred, I was
always tense and nervous, and I was overweight. My
solution for these ills was assorted pills. Instead of following
doctor's orders to abstain from alcohol on days I felt a need
for pills, I washed them down with alcohol.

Thinking I was on the verge of death and knowing I was
unable to control shaking except by an overdose of pills and
as much scotch as I could get down, I finally gave in to the
doctor's insistence and went to the hospital for a complete
physical examination. He convinced me to go by assuring
me I would be there only a couple of days, he concluded his
pre-release conference with the statement that I had to stop
drinking. I mouthed words of compliance to please him, but
I was looking forward to getting out of the hospital to get a

good, stiff shot of scotch. Fortunately for me I had an understanding doctor and friends who believed in "tough love." They arranged for me to go to a rehab center for priests.

Repeatedly at AA meetings I heard "this is an honest program." I did not understand the meaning of the words for several months. Honesty is telling it like it is. At my first meeting I did not believe I was alcoholic; I went because I was pressured into it. Even though I didn't think about my long-standing habit of lying whenever it seemed useful.

A few weeks after returning from rehab, I had to have minor outpatient surgery. I was able to be honest and tell the doctor about my alcoholism. He gave me post-operative pain pills that were supposed to be non-addictive. With the honesty found in sobriety, I took the medication according to his prescription. I stopped taking the pills after 24 hours. Whether it came from programmed thinking or physical craving, I began to feel a need for more pills. I prayed to my higher power to help me stay sober. I wrapped myself in blankets, listened to AA tapes, and shook for two hours. This was a more intense attack of tremors than I had ever experienced before. This impressed me with the fragility of my new way of life. As I sat there shaking, afraid I might take a drink, I accepted the fact that my honesty had not been good enough. I needed to be open and genuinely share my total alcohol-related life with at least one other person. My sponsor had said this many times, but I had chosen to ignore the wisdom of his knowledge and experience and to do it my way.

I knew I had to be honest with myself and open with at least one other person besides my Higher Power. I had to come out of the closet and say "I'm gay." Once I made this decision and said the words in my mind, I began to relax and to regain my composure. To follow this new turn on my personal route to serenity, as soon as my hands were steady enough to hold a book, I got an AA directory and began trying to locate a gay AA meeting. I called the number in the directory for time and location of the meeting.

In keeping with my long-standing habit of being early for appointments, I arrived at the meeting an hour early. Nothing happens apart from the overall plan of the Higher Power. My early arrival gave me an opportunity to get acquainted with John, "coffee-maker for the month." He introduced me to members as they came in and talked about the importance of gay AA for gay alcoholics. By the time the meeting started, I felt like I was part of the group. There was a first step discussion for my benefit. The Twelve Steps of AA are the same regardless of who the alcoholics are and regardless of where they are discussing their common problem of alcoholism. There is one addition to gay AA that makes it vitally significant for me and for many other gay alcoholics who choose to attend gay AA meetings. At that meeting, for the first time in my life, I said publicly, "I'm gay."

Feeling free to talk about being gay, about the guilt and resentment that had grown into depression so deep that it had led to attempted suicide by an overdose of pills was the most relieving and freeing experience I had ever had. Guilt started when I was ten years old; my mother caught me and a thirteen year old friend in sex play. Guilt continued growing throughout my drinking career as a result of occasional one-night stands that I blamed on over-drinking. Resentment started when my seminary confessor urged me to drop out of the seminary after I told him about going to bed with a priest. I nourished my resentment by often asking myself, "Why me?" Guilt and resentment continued to grow in me until I accepted myself and was accepted by the gay AA group before whom I could safely say, "I'm an alcoholic. I'm gay."

At a gay meeting I can be open and honest about being both alcoholic and gay because most of the people there are also both alcoholic and gay. Straight alcoholics often react differently when a person talks about alcohol related problems with a heterosexual spouse than when a person talks about alcohol related problems with a homosexual lover.

Each of us is a unique creation of our Higher Power. Each of us must work out a personal program to stay sober: implementation of the basic statement "Don't drink and go to meetings," for me includes sponsor, home group, and number of meetings. My program requires regular attendance at three meetings a week and at least one gay meeting a month.

I now accept myself as my Higher Power created me. Everything my Higher Power created is good, including me, left-handed, gay, alcoholic priest. Through gay AA I came to be happy to be me, thankful to my Higher Power for the gift of life that is uniquely mine.

This article originally appeared in NALGAP News 10.1 (1988): 5-6. It is reprinted with permission.

SERENITY PRAYER HELPS DURING LATE PREGNANCY

Marilyn Voelker

Marilyn Voelker shows how the principles of recovery can be used in all life's situations.

"God grant me the serenity to accept the things I cannot change..."

The beautiful thing about the principles and the 12 steps of AA is their application to any situation of life. I used them to get through pregnancy. It surely qualifies as "cannot be changed."

After 24 years of marriage and the rearing of six children (aged 13-23), I was finally enjoying the reward of grandmothering two beautiful grandchildren. For the first time in all those years, I felt free to "do my own thing." Then, as so often happens, God let me know that my will was not His. I was pregnant!

Little had George and I known how seriously God would take us as we'd repeated our wedding "I do's" two months before. But, serious He was; this unexpected event was His seal of approval on that re-commitment.

Steps 1, 2, and 3 lead us: to acknowledge our powerlessness over a situation; to recognize God's greater power over us in that situation; and to accept without reservation, God's will for us in that situation.

These same principles enabled me to handle middle-aged pregnancy with a sense of joy. That's not to say, though, that acceptance came automatically 1, 2, 3. It vacillated as I more or less yoyoed (in tune to vomiting and nausea) from step to step.

All the while I was so-o-o tired. An army tank running with a Volkswagen motor aptly describes how I felt most of the time. To further complicate matters, MY motor already had 100,000 or more miles on it. "One day at a time thinking" was essential for serenity during this time.

As the months went on it became necessary to add crutches to my unstable and "pachydermish" bulk because of hip and pelvic structural damage. Even the one day at a time philosophy was too difficult by then to manage. "You need to focus short of a time frame," someone told me. COMPLETE ACCEPTANCE OF THE PRESENT MOMENT became my thought until delivery.

That I could handle and accept--the present moment. From this concept I also learned it's not necessarily activity on one's part but the ACT of surrender and acceptance that glorifies God. Therefore, despite my "marooned" condition I could still so God's work.

Luke 6:38 says, "Give and it will be given to you, full measure, pressed down, shaken together, running over..."

True to His word, God gave a full measure in return for my once riotous will. A beautiful son, Jesse Nhan, was given to us. He is as his name signifies, "God's special gift" and "a thousand blessings."

This article originally appeared in Chalice *10.6 (1984): 2. It is reprinted with permission.*

RECOVERY IN THE BAHA'I COMMUNITY

Christina Zahn

*Many people have difficulty with AA
For some, this attitude comes from a
desire to continue drinking. But others,
such as Christina Zahn, find full,
spiritual recovery outside AA*

Alcohol was something that had always been a part of my life. I don't remember anytime when it was not used. When I was a child, it was primarily used as medication when I got sick. My father would keep raisins in the bottom of a whiskey bottle and when I was sick he gave them to me to eat. One of my early memories included climbing on top of the cabinet where the alcohol and other medicines were kept, specifically Contact and Vicks 44 (at that time, it contained codeine). I don't remember taking the Contact, but I would play with them like opening them up because of all the pretty colors, however the Vicks was much different. I would drink it from the bottle because I liked the taste and the warm feeling it gave me. This occurred between the ages of 5 and 8 years old. If wine was served, I almost always had a small cordial glass full. That was also the case with sloe gin fizzes. I also liked the head of a beer and, of course, the fruit served with mixed drinks.

Somewhere in my early teens I would sneak to the basement and take beer from the refrigerator and drank it quickly so as not to get caught (probably this is where I learned to chug). Also whenever my aunt and uncle went out for an evening I would get into the liquor cabinet, taking small amounts of just about everything and mixing it together so it would not look like any was being taken. My first drunk was when I was 14, it was at my niece's wedding.

My nephew who was the same age and I kept getting into the keg. I ended up with no ill effects, when most everyone else ended up either sick or with a hangover. The next drunk I had was at a New Year's Eve party when I was 17. I don't remember most of the party so I figure I had blacked out. Of the alcohol I used I believed I did so primarily because of the taste, not so much for the effect, however, I now believe it was a little of both. My preferences really never were for beer, but for vodka and whiskey.

College was a new experience altogether and I really let go. I always had a stash of liquor in the dorm room and used it almost daily. One thing I had read about several years before getting to college was the Baha'i Faith and it was something I wanted to check out. From the spiritual background I came from (Episcopal), I had read the Bible on a regular basis, but I had too many questions that the priests simply could not answer. It seemed to be a coincidence that a Baha'i lived next to me in the dorm, and Rhea gave me a lot of information and the books I read seemed to give me the answers to my questions. I knew by November, 1976 that I wanted to be a Baha'i, and had actually declared my belief in Baha'u'llah, however, I had a problem and I recognized it (although I had no intention of quitting at that time), and a variety of other crises. Rather than give up the alcohol I gave up the Faith. At that point I began drinking quite heavily, and that lasted at least the entire winter term at school. This is a period of time that I have very little memory, and what I do remember is related to my alcohol use and the couple of times I used marijuana. I even went and joined a sorority to fit in. I realize now that most everyone in the Gang was concerned about my behavior. For the sorority it was all natural/normal and expected stuff. I think that was part of my attraction to that segment of society.

By spring term, I knew I needed to become a Baha'i (1977). At that point, I felt that I could give up the alcohol, however in the living situation I had gotten myself into and what was going on in the family, I just wasn't strong enough to handle it, but of course, I wasn't about to admit it either. I did go for a short period without drinking, but I got started again. By the second year of school the alcohol problem worsened, and so did my grades. As I try to look at that year also, it is not very clear. I do remember Kathe and Sally, two women in my college dorm, confronting me about my use, but I don't think I really took them seriously.

As a Baha'i I was bound by Baha'i law, and alcohol is strongly prohibited. As a result, I could have lost my administrative rights, basically when rights are removed the individual cannot participate in community activities unless they are public events. This includes voting, serving on committees, attending Feasts, etc. However, this is not a rash decision by the National Spiritual Assembly. Ample opportunity is given to the individual to correct their infraction of the laws. Rights are not easily taken away either, and the Local Spiritual Assembly does not have authority to remove them, that is left to the National Spiritual Assembly. Being a new Baha'i I did not know this. Rhea, a dear friend, approached me about my drinking and her concern that if I did not go to the Assembly, she would. I did talk to someone in East Lansing and the reaction I received was very loving and out of true concern. I am not sure if that is where the road to recovery began or not, but I will never forget about how good I felt after. A period of abstinence soon followed. The way I rationalized it was, and I think part of this came from the talk I had with the

Assembly member, that I am human and not perfect, as long as I was conscious of the problem and willing to work on it, I would eventually recover. There was always a lot of prayer. I stopped counting how long ago it has been since I stopped drinking, but it was about four or five years after I became a Baha'i, so I try to count backwards if someone is interested.

The way I gave up alcohol was gradually, it was the only way I knew how to cope, as I gained new coping skills my need for the alcohol diminished. I went from a point where I used it daily, had a short period of abstinence, then some crisis would happen and I would drink start drinking again. As time went by the time of drinking shortened and the periods of abstinence lengthened to the point where towards the end I would have maybe a drink a year, and then it was no longer necessary. I remember that last year of wanting a drink and figured I had gone at least a year, why bother. Today the smell of most alcohol turns my stomach and I have little desire to use it any more at all. Occasionally the urge will be there, but I have been able to substitute it with a nonalcoholic malt beverage and/or the carbonated juices. Those seem to do the trick. Foods cooked with alcohol I can do without, the flavor comes straight through and ruins the meal.

I believe that there is a point where a person stops recovering and has recovered. That is the point where the behavior is so changed that the old behavior isn't even considered an option any longer. Unfortunately, for most people we quite often replace one negative behavior for another.

I am still in recovery from bulimia, and it's a wonderful feeling not to be intent on getting rid of most everything or feeling so guilty. I have recovered from a depression that lasted for many years, it is a wonderful feeling just to enjoy my life and the opportunities that are out there, along with taking risks once in a while. I am still working on my most serious addiction--food. This one has posed a big problem for me, but I feel I am on the right step and getting the right treatment to work on it. For this one I call on the support of God, my doctor, therapist, and friends.

A note about the twelve steps. Personally, I have a lot of difficulty with them, especially the first step. I cannot accept powerlessness over my addictions, because for me the power comes from within. It's all a process. Once I am truly beginning recovery, only I can make the choice to recover and do all that I can to follow through with that decision, and at that point I believe intervention is given to help me make it the rest of the way. I know the 12-step approach has helped many people, and working in intervention both as a volunteer and professional, when the need arises, I do not hesitate to refer people to a 12-step program. However, if they have difficulty with the program, there are other options within the community to refer them to. About the greatest thing I take from the 12-steps is taking things one day at a time.

I don't know if any of this can help you or not, but it is the basics of my story. There has been some discussion of whether or not I was actually an alcoholic, some people have stated that unless I had used the 12-steps to recover I could not have been an alcoholic. However, I know what went on in my life and how difficult recovery was, I am a recovered alcoholic. And none of this could have been accomplished without my Faith and very special friends who stuck with me through it all.

This essay is revised from a letter written to the editor and is reprinted with permission of the author.

I'M A MEMBER OF Al-Anon

Father Mike

The alcoholic's family and friends, like the alcoholic, are powerless over alcohol. Al-Anon offers them a program of recovery so that they can find serenity whether or not the alcoholic recovers. Fr. Mike's story is an example.

I am Father Mike. I'm powerless over alcohol. My life has been unmanageable. I'm a member of Al-Anon.

I like to introduce myself in that way because it reminds me why I am here. This is my second NCCA convention. I attended the convention in Boston in 1973 and while I was there I enjoyed meeting all the wonderful people who were there. I'm happy to recognize a number of those people here. I'd like to start by telling you one experience that I had in Boston which may not have been noticed by anyone else, but it has been significant in my life.

I went to the first session in Boston and one of the priests there greeted me something like this: "You seem awfully young to be here for the program. You are not an alcoholic, are you?" When I told him that I was not an alcoholic he looked surprised and asked, "Then why are you here?" When I said "I am a member of Al-Anon," I thought he would swallow the cigar he was smoking. He gave me the same confused look I get at a lot of AA meetings and Al-Anon meetings, especially when I am wearing my clerical collar. When I go in clericals invariably someone will walk up to me and say, "It's good to see you here, Father. I'm glad to see that you are taking an interest in us people." When I say I am a member if Al-Anon, I get more surprised looks.

My reason for being in Al-Anon is that I had to take that first step and admit that I was powerless over alcohol, that my life had become unmanageable. It isn't easy to say that, and I don't enjoy saying it, but I have to because it is part of my life, and in a group like this one I stand here full of gratitude.

Already in the seminary I used to be asked why I kept going to these meetings. I always said because unless I did I probably would never become a priest, I would never hold to my vocation if I discontinued these meetings. Through Al-Anon I want you to know I have found a lot more meaning in my life.

Let me briefly tell you a little about my past and how I got into Al-Anon. You will see what it means to me today. Thinking of my past means thinking of being loved. I have been loved by so many. Certainly I have been loved by God; my life has been filled with many gentle experiences of God's love. I like the title of Father John Powell's book He Touched Me. God has touched me in many ways in my life and the touch of God is one of the experiences of love. It tells me that I'm o.k., that things are fine, that when I do wrong I'm forgiven. I experience the love of God in many ways and I believe I have experienced that love from childhood.

For most of us I think the first experience of love is in the home. I was very much loved by my mother and father and I believe that I experienced God through a family that is very close, a family which gave me two brothers and four sisters. God has come into my life through the love I experienced in my family.

Alcohol has been a part of my life; the alcoholism of a loved one has been something in my background that has made things a little difficult for me. Everyone, of course, has difficulties. One of the things that I am grateful to the program for is this: I can go to an AA meeting or an Al-Anon meeting and there see people who are growing. Then I come back to the rectory, where I meet someone with many problems who is not growing, because he does not have a program.

My dad is an alcoholic. It took me a long time to realize that. Before I speak of my home or background let me share with you something that occurred on my way to the airport as I started for Los Angeles. My driver was a parishioner, a young man who asked me where I was going. I told him the kind of meeting this would be and he said: "That sounds like a very interesting conference." Then he told me that his father had died of alcoholism. During the past year many friends asked him what happened to his father. He has to tell them that he died. They express their sympathy and then bring up the next question: "What did he die of?" When he tells them it was alcoholism they look confused and upset. But he said that doesn't bother him, because no matter how they look at him, he loved his father. That is what I want to say by way of preface. I love my father, and I hope you remember that regardless of what I now have to say.

As I grew up in a good home I idolized my father. He was idealistic; he was energetic, very active in our school and church activities. Alcoholism was not part of my childhood really, not the rough part. My father was a man who drank whenever he was with friends of the family, though he probably did not drink as much as some of the people who were our friends.

As I grew older I began to recognize problems in our home. I was in high school when the family trials began to surface, and though we had a very close and loving family after each summer vacation I returned to the seminary a little bit more upset. I attended a high school seminary and possibly I glorified my family in the eyes of the students and faculty, made them a little better than they really were. Then when I returned home for the Christmas or summer vacation I would not find them exactly as I had pictured them. They did not measure up to my expectations and I would come back to the school a disappointed young man. It took me a long time to recognize that alcohol was at least part of the problem, and part of id was my inability to understand what was happening.

Then a real change came about when I graduated from college. I went home and I must have had several run-ins with my father in ways that I did not understand. The last day of the vacation I was arguing politics with my father-- not an unusual thing at the time--but I noticed he was repeating the same thing over and over, maybe as often as fifteen times. I said, "Dad, you are not making any sense; you are drunk again." With that I left the room. Those were my last words to him before I left for the seminary.

What I did then was to heap on guilt. I heaped guilt on my father, but I also felt guilt in myself, for I knew that I had been disrespectful of my father. I talked about the incident to one of the priests at the seminary. I told him that I was upset with myself for getting mad at my dad. He asked me if I had ever considered the possibility that my father was an alcoholic. I looked at him and said, "No, he's not an alcoholic; he just drinks too much." That's how I viewed my father. It was hard for me at that time to see my father drunk. He was such a great man in my sight. He loved the blacks, he was a leader in our neighborhood, he was very intelligent in matters of politics and religion, even though he was not highly educated. I was proud of him and it hurt me to see him not in full control of his life.

I was not in control of mine either, but in that frame of mind I entered First Theology. A few things happened to me in the course of that year. I was asked to take part in a musical that we put on every year, and the director was beside himself trying to get me to relax. "Can't you smile?" he would say, but I couldn't. I was up tight.

One day I met a fellow student in the hall. "Are you looking for a fight?" he asked. I asked, "What do you mean?" "Look at your hands," he said. My hands were actually clenched into fists. I was afraid to put myself forward; I found myself copping out on a lot of work that I could have done. I was not doing what I should have been doing in my studies; I accepted myself as mediocre; the image I had of myself was not going to get me anywhere.

I returned home from the seminary that year to find things different from what I had always known them to be. I could not exactly put my finger on the difference but I knew something had changed. I mentioned this to my sister and she said the difference was that my mother had joined Al-Anon. I did not find the arguing going on that I had remembered. I asked what is Al-Anon, and my sister said, "Why don't you ask mother? She is the one who belongs."

Her explanation was a good one. "Well, your father is an alcoholic." At that point I recalled that the priest at the seminary had asked me if I had given any thought to the possibility that my father was an alcoholic. I became involved in Al-Anon and before returning to the seminary for another year I had some plans. I wanted to try to get father sober.

Now you have all heard the stories of how brilliant people are going to get someone to stop drinking, like pouring the booze down the drain, etc. Well, I came up with a brilliant idea of how to cure an alcoholic. My dad was drinking one night in his customary way. He was a beer drinker; I rarely saw him get drunk, but he was drinking pretty much around the clock. He had about two quarts of beer in the refrigerator and I knew he would sit in front of the TV and drink the whole bit. I got a glass and started to drink with him. I figured if he would drink only half the supply he would get only half-drunk. That was my bright way of keeping an alcoholic from getting drunk.

Needless to say he was provoked at me and after I had my first couple of glasses he ordered me to put my glass away. He did not want me to have any more of his beer.

I tried another thing that summer just before I went back to help him get sober. I thought what I would do was to talk to him about it. The occasion was a card party we had at our home. We had a number of relatives in and we played cards into the wee hours of the morning. The following morning, Saturday, I invited dad to go with me for a ride. I got him into the car and I was planning to ask him a question. He would have to answer it. "Dad, I'd like to ask you about your drinking..." (I was going to say, "Why do you drink so much?"). Before I even got the word "drinking" out of my mouth he said, "I don't want to talk about it. Let's go and have a beer." So we went to the bar and had a beer.

The seed had been planted and it seemed that year at school that everything had a bearing on alcoholism. Information about alcoholism came from all kinds of sources. I did not get it directly from the curriculum but I did get much from a friend. He came to my room and told me: "I have a problem; I have some bad news from home." He told me about his parents, that both of them were alcoholics, both of them had been taken to the hospital for treatment at the same time. That was in October. Around Thanksgiving we talked again and he told me how great things were going for his family. He was enthusiastic about Alcoholics Anonymous.

Then he told me he was doing a paper on Alcoholism. He knew about my dad's problem and lent me some of his books. One of them was the Big Book <u>Alcoholics Anonymous</u>. He gave me five or six other books. In a matter of a week or so I had read them all and everything I could get my hands on about alcoholism. I resolved to become an expert in this thing. It was really an interesting discovery.

I decided to try to take an independent study course on alcoholism under the psychology professor in order to familiarize myself with this problem and thus be of help to others. He gave me a number of assignments to do including a long term paper. By January I had done all my research and I told him I was ready to start writing. But he did not think so. "Before you write a word," he said, "I want you to attend at least three AA meetings." The next night I attended my first AA meeting and I was impressed. The first thing I heard was a man telling my father's story. It was identical right up to the sobriety part. That had not yet come to my dad. The next week I heard a young man two years my junior tell his story, and it scared me. It sounded a little bit like me, except that I did not have the drinking experiences--but the attitude, the way he was living--that scared me.

I kept going back for some weeks. Then someone asked me "Why don't you go to Al-Anon?" I started at once to attend one AA meeting and one Al-Anon meeting a week and continued to do this for almost a year.

By this time I had finished my paper for the term. The professor thought it was good enough to present on "Thesis Day" at the seminary. Then two of our men came up from New York City to hear me talk about alcoholism, two men who are in the program and are here today. They invited

me to the conference in Boston, and that is how I got there-
-and here.

Somewhere I left the point I was going to make. When
the priest at Boston asked me why I was going to Al-Anon
I said I was a member of Al-Anon. That was the first time
I ever said that. Always before I had said I go to the
meetings because I am doing a research paper. Now I could
say I am a member or Al-Anon.

Now allow me to tell you how I got into it and what it
has done for me. And even had I become a priest without
it I know that I would not be happy in my choice of a
vocation; I could not have been happy making a decision in
the state of mind that I was in. I was confused and the
confusion came between love and hate, or love and
disrespect. When I didn't know how to love my father I
discovered that I didn't know how to love myself or how to
love God. I didn't know how to love anything. I needed to
learn how to love. All it meant before was a good-sounding
word.

So in Al-Anon I think I learned the meaning of love. I
learned that it meant self-respect, not being afraid to be who
I am. I learned that it meant accepting other persons as
they are, recognizing them for who they are. For that I am
most grateful to Al-Anon. I am no longer up-tight. I have
a freedom about myself. I have become much more
understanding and compassionate towards people with all
problems. I did not understand homosexuality, bad
marriages, experiencing the loss of a dear one, terminal
illness. I learned to have compassion through Al-Anon. It
has meant a great deal in my ministry as a priest and I am
sure it has meant a great deal to many of you.

Here is another thing it has meant to me. Do you know
what we mean by "warm fuzzies?" These are the little
experiences of love that we see in a group. It's seeing

somebody that you once directed to AA celebrating his first anniversary of sobriety; it's seeing a family get together whose home was shattered by alcoholism, now reuniting in love. These are things we are blessed in seeing.

And finally I am grateful to Al-Anon for the opportunity to share with all of you people. If anyone has ever questioned whether a priest should go to Al-Anon I will always say "Yes," because then you can know an alcoholic, you can know the people you have to deal with. For me it has meant a way of life. The twelve steps are a way that I have come to know and have learned to live. I thank you for the opportunity to be with all of you through Al-Anon.

This article originally appeared in NCCA Blue Book 29 (1977): 156-161. It is reprinted with permission.

For Further Reading on
Stories of Recovery

Allen, C. (1978). I'm Black & I'm Sober. Minneapolis, Minnesota: CompCare Publications.

Allen, the daughter of a minister, tells the story of her addiction and recovery.

(1973). Came to Believe: The Spiritual Adventure of AA as Experienced by Individual Members. New York: Alcoholics Anonymous World Services, Inc.

A collection of first person accounts of how the spirituality of AA works in their lives.

Casey, F. (1975). Relationship Between Religious Life and AA. NCCA Blue Book, 30, 109-141.

Brother Casey presents his "concept of spirituality and the concept of a religious life; what community is about and what the fellowship of Alcoholics Anonymous is about." Comparisons are made between AA and Christianity. The essay ends with comments from several brothers and nuns.

Chabernaud, L. (1989). Drugs, AIDS, and a Higher Power. PWA Coalition Newsline, 44, 52.

In this poem, Chabernaud, a person with AIDS, explains what he learned about drugs in treatment. He ends the poem by mentioning the relationship he has with his higher power.

Charest, J. (May/June 1984). An Agnostic Works It Out. Recovery, 14-15.

Charest tells how he overcame his agnosticism while in treatment.

(February 1987). Coming Home: The Experiences of an Adult Child of an Alcoholic. Sisters Today, 352-355.

The anonymous nun who wrote this article explains what it is like to have an alcoholic father.

Dowling, R. M. (April 1985). Journey of an Adult Child. Sisters Today, 482-485.

Dowling summarizes the main points of Janet Geringer Woititz's "Adult Child of Alcoholics" as she tells of her own recovery as an adult child of an alcoholic. Part of her recovery involved inpatient treatment and aftercare. Special mention is made in the change in her relationship with God.

Earle M. (1989). Physician, Heal Thyself! 35 Years of Adventures in Sobriety by an AA 'Old Timer'. Minneapolis, Minnesota: CompCare Publishers.

A medical doctor tells the story of his addiction and recovery through AA

Eleanor M. (1989). What We Could Not Do For Ourselves. Box 1980: The AA Grapevine, Inc., 45(11), 8-10.

Eleanor, an alcoholic nun who recovered through AA, describes her first meeting.

(February 1987). A Funny Thing Happened on the Way to Unemployment. Sisters Today, 349-351.

The anonymous nun tells about how having a car became an obsession with her and about how losing the car helped her better understand the AA principles of "a spiritual awakening," "acceptance," and "surrender."

(May 1987). I Am an Alcoholic Priest. Catholic Digest, 98-100.

Writing under the pseudonym "Father Anonymous" because he respects the traditions of AA, the author tells the story of when he met an elderly parishioner at her first AA meeting to explain the disease concept of alcoholism. He concludes his article by stressing that "True kindness makes an alcoholic face the consequences of his drinking."

Jeanne E. (1987). Women and Spirituality. Center City, MN: Hazelden.

Jeanne describes some of the special issues which face some women in accepting a higher power. The booklet ends with five testimonials from women who describe the higher powers in their lives.

Mel B ([1974]). Is There Life After Sobriety?: How An AA Member Sees the Problems and Challenges of Living. Toledo, OH: by the author.

This book is a collection of Mel B.'s articles that appeared in the Grapevine, AA's monthly magazine. Articles on both spiritual and non-spiritual issues in recovery are included in the book.

(1970). A Members Eye View of Alcoholics Anonymous. New York, New York: Alcoholics Anonymous World Services, Inc.

In part, the anonymous AA member explains that the impact of "AA therapy" is that the steps are "reports of action taken rather than rules not to be broken under pain of drunkenness." The wording of the steps is compared to the ten commandments.

Ollerman, W. (June 1983). The Help that Came Too Late...A Clergy Widows Story. Record, 1-3.

The author describes her husband's addiction and alcohol related death.

Pastor Paul (1973). The 13th American. Elgin, IL: David C. Cook Publishing Company.

Paul, an alcoholic who recovered through AA, presents his experience, strength, and hope in this autobiography.

Paul H. (1987). Things My Sponsor Taught Me. Center City, MN: Hazelden.

Paul H. offers an interpretation of various aspects of the AA program. One section is devoted to "higher powers and prayer."

Pfau, R., & Hirshberg, A. (1958). Prodigal Shepherd. Indianapolis: SMT Guide.

The book is an autobiography of Father Pfau, an alcoholic priest who recovered through AA.

Smith, B. (1950). Last Major Talk of Doctor Bob Smith. Cleveland, OH: Alcoholics Anonymous.

Smith, a co-founder of AA, talks about early AA. He gives special attention to the spirituality of AA.

Stromsten, A. e. (1982). Recovery: Stories of Alcoholism and Survival. New Brunswick: Rutgers Center of Alcohol Studies.

The book is a collection of testimonials of people who have recovered from alcoholism. Of special interest are the stories of two clergyman: David W. and Vernon J.

Walker, R. (nd). For Drunks Only: One Man's Reaction to Alcoholics Anonymous. Center City, MN: Hazelden.

Walker, an early AA member and author of Twenty Four Hours a Day, presents this story as to what it was like, what happened, and what it is like today.

Walther, L., Sears, M., & Curran, J. (1970). The Woman Alcoholic. NCCA Blue Book, 22, 79-92.

This panel was designed to help the conference participants to better understand alcoholism in women. The panelists were all alcoholics who recovered through AA.

(1981). The Way Back: The Stories of Gay and Lesbian Alcoholics, Third Edition. Washington, D.C.: Whitman-Walker Clinic, Inc.

The ten stories in this book are written in the style of those stories found in Alcoholics Anonymous. Five of the stories are by gay men. Five are by lesbians.

Weems, R. (May, 1987). This Mother's Daughter. Essence, 75-76, 150, 152, 154.

Weems, a minister of the African Methodist Episcopal Church, describes her relationship with her alcoholic mother.

SPIRITUAL ISSUES
IN RECOVERY

THE PUZZLE OF AA

Griffith Edwards

AA is a puzzle because logically, it ought not to work. In trying to unravel the puzzle, Griffith Edwards explains the spiritual nature of AA recovery.

Alcoholics Anonymous continues to grow and to puzzle psychiatrists by breaking all the rules of psychotherapy yet producing some outstanding successes.

Hospitals have their failures, but the outlook for this particular man seemed so entirely hopeless that before he was discharged his case was presented at a case conference for psychiatric social workers as an illustration of the fact that there are alcoholics who simply cannot be helped. Psychotherapy had been tried but it failed because he could not form any useful relationship with the therapist--he put on a front of polite unconcern. He was given Antabuse, a drug which makes a man nauseated if he drinks after taking the tablet and which is often a useful aid in the early days of sobriety--this man simply palmed the tablets and slipped out to the pub. A young PSW student became very involved in this case and spent hours talking with the wife and still more hours in trying to get the family rehoused and the man working again--the patient was politely grateful but viewed his own problems as distantly as he would have those of the man in the moon.

In his early 30s, this man seemed to be heading for the bombed sites and the surgical spirit drinking schools. He did not turn up again until five years later, when he dropped in at the hospital just to tell us how he was getting on. He had by now been in several other hospitals and he had also been in prison. For the last year, however, he had been completely sober, and he had bought himself some very smart clothes as an outward sign of inner change. He was, he claimed, also happy and contented, holding down a job, and planning to take his family on the first holiday they had ever had together. He was going to an Alcoholics Anonymous meeting every night of the week, and much of his spare time was being spent helping other alcoholics.

Any psychiatrist who had in the course of psychotherapy produced such changes would have been pleased with the result. The man's whole ability to function had altered for the better. He could now handle relationships with other people and he could deal with situations of frustration and conflict which, when we first knew him, he could only respond to by drinking. AA, he said, was the answer.

Historically, AA was an offshoot of the Oxford Group. Although this origin seems now usually to be forgotten, the ancestral influence of evangelical Christianity can still be identified in most AA practices. AA started in May, 1935, when Bill W., an alcoholic stock broker from New York, was desperately looking for help and somehow, as a result of dialing a wrong number, managed to get hold of Bob S., and alcoholic doctor from Akron. They got together that evening, and by the following year they had been joined by a handful of other alcoholics who had regular meetings for bible readings, discussion and self analysis. From this earliest stage "confession" was an important part of the activity, as was the idea of restitution. AA had from the start the characteristics of an action group: members were expected not only to talk about their problems but were also expected to do something about these problems and lead a certain sort of life. The link with the Oxford Group was severed in 1937, and since then AA has been completely independent of any affiliation.

By 1939, AA had about 100 members and by 1948 membership had grown to 40,000. The number of members at the present time is difficult to estimate. The movement became established in England soon after the war. In London and the Home Counties over 50 meetings are held each week. A commercial traveller could be fairly sure of being able to contact AA in any large town or city--from Exeter to Renfrew--in which he put up for the night. A visiting professor would find active groups in Oxford and in Cambridge. On holiday, whether in Jersey, Tipperary, or Stornoway, AA is still at hand.

There is a certain form of words with which the Chairman opens the meeting. He starts with "My name is Joe"--or Jack or Fred as the case may be--"and I'm an alcoholic." To be able to say "and I'm an alcoholic" without embarrassment, and perhaps sometimes it seems even with a certain inflection of pride, is the badge of the AA member.

Desolate Degradation

The evening's speaker goes on to give his life story. This is a confession, a catharsis, in which the audience, all of whom have themselves been through some similar experience of life, are able intensely to share. The story is likely to be told with sincerity and passion. The speaker tells probably of desolation and degradation and then, with a regularity that makes one feel that one is watching some primitive stylized dramatic form, comes the moment when the man joins AA, drags himself out of the gutter, and finds contented sobriety. There are infinite variations on the theme, but the basic flow of the story seems always to be the same. General discussion follows, and then comes tea and biscuits.

If an attempt is made to analyze the meetings, the analysis must somehow take account of the fact that, as in psychotherapy, it is not only the words which count, but the emotional interactions. However, a superficial content analysis would bring out one point so obvious that it must surely deserve attention: most of what is said is about drink and drinking.

With what at first appears to be boring reiteration, the meetings drive at the fact that alcoholism is a disease, an allergy, a disorder of metabolism, something akin to diabetes. Drinking story is told after drinking story, and at times the whole meeting seems to lean forward with vicarious pleasure as some particularly momentous drinking spree is described down to the last bottle and the last blackout. In these stories the danger of "the first drink" is stressed and stressed again, and there is a frequently repeated phrase about one drink being too many and one hundred not enough.

An alcoholic, according to the doctrine which is reiterated at these meetings, must accept his alcoholism as a physical fact, and if he refuses to accept this fact "and makes an experiment" he is beckoning disaster. Such a blunt and unsophisticated emphasis on drinking rather than on supposed underlying emotional causes of drinking is in contrast to the approach which the alcoholic is likely to encounter with many psychotherapists. Psychotherapists can even be found who make the statement that, basically, alcoholism has nothing to do with alcohol.

It would be wrong to suppose that AA gives no attention at all to problems other than the immediate problem of alcohol. Part of the time at a meeting may be spent in discussing "thinking." There is a phrase of admonition which is sometimes heard to the effect that "it's not your drinking but your stinking thinking," and it is held in AA that there are faulty attitudes which can be identified as "alcoholic thinking." For instance, the alcoholic is seen as a man who has a tendency to put the blame on others. He is always looking for excuses. He is someone who is always in a hurry, trying to do too much too soon, a fault which is corrected by the AA teaching that you keep sober "just for today." The individual is invited to search himself for a number of wrong headed stereotypes of reaction pattern.

Although there is now what amounts to a large body of uncodified doctrine--the host of familiar catch phrases that go to and fro at every AA meeting--the actual official doctrine remains small. There are Twelve Steps, which are the guide to AA organization.

The Twelve Steps are:

1. We admitted that we were powerless over alcohol--that our lives had become unmanageable.
2. Came to believe that a power greater than ourselves could restore us to sanity.
3. Made a decision to turn our will and our lives over to the care of God--as we understood Him.
4. Made a searching and fearless moral inventory of ourselves.
5. Admitted to God, to ourselves and to another human being the exact nature of our wrongs.
6. Were entirely ready to have God remove all these defects of character.
7. Humbly asked Him to remove our shortcomings.
8. Made a list of all persons we had harmed and became willing to make amends to them all.
9. Made direct amends to such people whenever possible, except when to do so would injure them or others.
10. Continued to take personal inventory and when we were wrong, promptly admitted it.
11. Sought through prayer and meditation to improve our conscious contact with God--as we

understood Him--praying only for knowledge of
His will for us and the power to carry that out.

12. Having had a spiritual awakening as the result of
the steps, we tried to carry this message to
alcoholics and practice these principles in all our
affairs.

On to the Spiritual

A feature of the twelve steps--as opposed to the
manifest content of any AA discussion--is that alcohol and
alcoholism are each only mentioned once while God is
mentioned five times. At American meetings, the Lord's
Prayer will often be said, but English AA puts a less
conscious emphasis on religion. A recurrent problem arises
in interpreting the twelve steps in such a way as to make
AA acceptable to the alcoholic who is not theistic, and
arguments go on around the "as we understood him", a
clause which seems to embrace even denying his existence.
Sometimes however an alcoholic who at first sees in AA
only a method of keeping dry, will later "go on to get the
spiritual side."

The Twelve Traditions lay down a simple framework for
organization and administration. Central control is to be
kept to a minimum. Groups are to avoid entanglements of
big funds, and AA is to be self supporting. Members are to
speak for themselves and not for AA. One of the reasons
it has burgeoned into an international organization seems to
be the right balance has been struck between central control
and group autonomy.

None of this provides the whole explanation of how a
man who has failed completely to benefit from everything
which psychiatry could provide, should come back five years
later sober and wearing a new suit and saying, "I don't let

things get on my nerves the way they used to do." AA eschews psychiatric jargon, and yet some effort at interpretation in terms of group dynamics seems necessary for complete understanding although not for its functioning.

The most immediately apparent fact about the dynamics of AA is that the AA group is a group without a leader. Group therapy, which like AA has burgeoned since the war, has as its uncodified first step the assumption that group therapists are the prerequisite of group therapy. The training of the group therapist has given him awarenesses and skills which are used by him to direct and interpret the processes of group interaction. Yet AA has no trained person to control its interactions, and all the mistakes which the trained therapist would wish the group to avoid, the AA group presumably goes straight ahead and makes. All the uncontrolled and devious manifestations of projected aggression and projected anxiety presumably leap like lightning about the room.

The absence of a leader tempts the psychiatrist to try to detect substitute and symbolic leaders. AA itself can be conceived of as an abstract "good object." One could erect a number of other hypotheses: that God is the group's symbolic leader, the chairman plays the role of therapist, that Bob S. and Bill W. have in some ways taken on symbolic stature, but the fact is that AA works through undirected group processes. The absence of a therapist may in part be responsible for the strength of the group cohesion: there is no father-protector to hold the group together and for this reason if the group is to survive (and it badly wants to survive) anxieties must be very quickly dealt with. The absence of a therapist seems also sometimes to result in anxieties being repressed rather than resolved: there are taboo subjects, such as homosexuality.

Another interesting aspect of AA dynamics is that interaction is not limited to the meeting. In conventional group therapy the therapist hopes to work through a network of transferences and counter transferences and verbal interactions, and he hopes very much to avoid acting out. Aggression must be at a verbal level rather than an exchange of blows, and sympathy must be verbal rather than a loan of money. His patients gather in his room, and he will probably feel that the therapeutic process will work best if they go their ways until the next meeting.

In AA the state of affairs is very different. A well established AA member will accept responsibility as sponsor for the newly joined member, and will go round to the new member's house, and spend hours talking to him over cups of tea. An AA member has even been known to try to stop a divorce by going round to give a solicitor a lecture on the disease concept of alcoholism. The sponsor is not held back by any of the qualms about involvement which might inhibit the well trained social worker. But even in AA the older hands will caution against over involvement and will insist that no one can be helped until that person really wants help.

AA is not simply a crutch which offers the abnormal personality mere support in contrast to psychotherapeutic processes which actually correct the abnormality, although there are indeed occasional cases where AA does no more than support a man in a chronic state of neurotic maladjustment. Alas, psychiatry can often do no better. Sobriety itself, however achieved, can sometimes allow a spontaneous maturation of personality, but AA seems often to exert a specific and positive psychotherapeutic effect by offering a man what is at first the experience of an accepting group. Experience of the group later breaks down into a network of individual relationships which may often be the first warm and meaningful relationships which the alcoholic has been able to experience. AA is seldom able to help the drifting, rootless man who has very limited powers to form relationships of any sort: the skidrow alcoholic is as poor a candidate for AA as he is for psychotherapy. There are also people with a rather introverted nature who find AA meetings disconcerting, and who feel more able to work out their problems with an individual doctor.

AA in London cooperates very successfully with the medical profession and the experienced AA sponsor will not infrequently persuade an alcoholic to seek psychiatric help. In some mental hospitals regular AA meetings are held.

AA thus has a double importance: firstly as a therapeutic organization of energy and ubiquity, and secondly as a puzzle of extreme theoretical interest. Therapy without therapists, sponsors manifesting unashamed involvement, groups demanding repression, emphasis on the symptom rather than the disease--and all this producing therapeutic successes sometimes of startling brilliance. If we could understand AA we should in the process come to understand a great deal about human interaction.

This article originally appeared in New Society 3.87 (1964): 10-11. It is reprinted with permission.

RECOVERY

Sister Florence

Sister Florence argues that "staying sober is not really as simple as saying 'I'm not going to take a drink.'" Recovery is a process that needs to be learned. AA provides the type of reinforcement which the alcoholic needs to learn the recovery process.

...This afternoon I'm going to talk to you on a subject that I think many of you here know something about, and some of you know quite a lot about, I'm sure. And that is the subject of recovery. The material that we're going to talk about will touch on old learning as well as new learning regarding alcoholism. Some real problems of the alcoholic will be cited and considered as well as some helpful ones to reinforce the sobriety that many of us enjoy one day at a time. In this lecture, which has to do with learning, the main thing that we're learning about is how to stay sober. When we say "sober," we mean sober by abstaining from pills as well as abstaining from alcohol. Some, while they say they haven't had a drink in six weeks or three months, have in fact been taking pills, which is eating the chemical as opposed to drinking liquid chemical. So, if a person is substituting one for the other, there is still alcoholism present and there is a problem. So whether it's a liquid or a solid, it is still a problem of alcoholism.

We have to learn to stay sober because I think most of us, many of us at least, are teachers, and we know that appropriate and inappropriate behavior is learned. Staying sober is not really as simple as saying, "I'm not going to take a drink," or "I'm not going to take valium," or "I'm not going to take Librium," or whatever your thing is. If it were that simple, then no one would ever have to go into treatment centers and no one would need any kind of reinforcement, particularly the reinforcement which many of us here are familiar with as Alcoholics Anonymous.

Staying sober has to be learned. It's a learning process and it has nothing to do with will power. As a matter of fact, it has quite a bit to do with "won't" power. It is that I won't take a drink, that I won't take a pill. It has very little to do with making "never again" statements. We're not really impressed with never again statements. Never again is too long a time to deal with. I think most of us know that we have only today. We're not sure about how much longer. So we're going to talk about things we can learn quickly and easily; there are simple principles of learning.

We learn quickly and easily things that we can use continually for a long period of time. We learn quickly and easily things that have been drilled into us when we were very young. We learn quickly and easily things that we catch onto very fast, something we have a flair for or enjoy doing very much. We also learn easily things that give us immediate pleasure and that we enjoy doing over again. These are simple principles of learning and they will help a person with a drinking problem to stay sober if they're allowed to filter down to that level. Usually when a patient leaves a treatment center, he feels very well. He often says he's feeling better than he has felt in a number of years and he can enjoy the simple pleasures of life--seeing a movie, enjoying a meal, watching a television program. One thing usually mentioned when a patient leaves a treatment center is that he doesn't really have the desire to drink. This is not too uncommon. The prevailing attitude is very often "I won't take a drink" or "I won't take a pill" because he feels then that he understands the illness of alcoholism, and he knows he can't tolerate one drink or one pill with safety.

All of this is understood usually on an intellectual level. But it has not necessarily filtered down to the gut level.

We might know of some people who got drunk on the way home from treatment centers, or we might know of some who stayed sober for a couple of weeks, or for a couple of months. And we wonder how this happens. We can't understand why the person so quickly went back to drinking.

Many people in the fellowship of Alcoholics Anonymous have never been in for treatment. So there are other ways of grasping sobriety. Some people are in hospitals, ten, twelve times. Some are in hospitals as often as twenty-six times. These are what we call professional patients. They tend to make a hobby or an occupation of trying different treatment facilities, hoping maybe the next time to hear something they did not hear before. This is why we're thinking about the learning theory.

Hopefully, it will be easy to understand how a person can have relapses and go back to drinking because maybe those things haven't gotten down to the feeling level and the gut level, where they're really effective, they're really making an impact on his behavior. A very simple example of a learning theory is that most of us when we were in high school studied history of algebra or chemistry, but unless we teach one of these subjects, or unless we're still in that field, it's very easy to forget that subject matter. Some of us don't use facts about history, or algebra, or chemistry and therefore, we've forgotten a lot of those things. Just to ask you a few questions, could you tell me for instance, your license plate number that was on your car last year? Or could you tell me you telephone number of maybe two residences ago or two convents ago or two rectories ago? Just for a quick recall. This might be difficult.

These are not things used by us frequently. We have a tendency to forget and therefore there's a difficulty remembering. The same thing is true with our learning theory. We do remember, for instance, things like nursery rhymes because we associate happy days with childhood and happy circumstances of learning nursery rhymes. We do remember things that were drilled into us. Sisters worked very hard to help us remember our prayers when we were young. Later on, we were taught the Gettysburg Address and were able to recite that verbatim. That learning was drilled into us; we went over our multiplication tables, many, many times in grade school. So those things were drilled into us.

Old learning represents the things we have heard over and over again. They're the old attitudes and the old concepts that society has taught us over a long period of time. Some old learning facts in regard to alcoholism include that having alcoholism indicates a sign of a weak character. I'm sure that many of you have heard this old type of learning. You've heard of the type of person who's called the town drunk. He's also been referred to as a Skid Row bum. That's the old theory, that alcoholism is a sign of a weak character.

Another one is that anyone with will power should be able either to take a drink or not take a drink but an alcoholic cannot do that. The alcoholic always takes it. Another one is that we should be able to leave it alone. The alcoholic can't necessarily leave it alone. Then, some people will say, "One drink won't hurt you." That's music to the ears of an alcoholic who wants to drink. Just one drink won't hurt you. And another old learning theory is that no one gets drunk is he doesn't want to. I think some of us know that alcoholics get drunk many times when they don't intend to. And then the last is that the immediate pleasure that should come to us from taking a drink releases all tensions, lowers the anxiety level and does a lot of other things that are not necessarily true. Often after that drink is taken we wind up making spectacles of ourselves in public.

Somewhere along the line new thinking sets in and this gives us pleasure now. What usually follows is a great deal of distress and pain and remorse and guilt. Then we have to think of better ways, not necessarily of the old learning anymore, but we have to put new learning in its place. So what are some of the things that we consider learning?

You hear much these days about the fact that alcoholism is an illness. That's the first new learning theory. That alcoholism is an illness, it is a treatable disease. We can recover, and a number of us in this room are arrested alcoholics. It has three main characteristics: it's progressive, it's chronic, and it usually carries with it that "blind spot," because the longer a person continues to use the chemical the more difficult it becomes to see this. This is difficult learning. Any learning that affects us in a personal way sometimes can become very difficult.

Then, the second new learning theory is that regardless of will power, strength of character, or adequate personality, the alcoholic is unable to react normally to chemicals. The chemicals in the body of an alcoholic do not metabolize properly and bizarre behavior sets in. Crazy phone calls are made, whereas if the person is sober, crazy things are not being done. We have to keep reminding ourselves that there is a better way to live and there are better theories to put into practice in our lives, so we have to keep talking to ourselves about these things.

Alcoholics are usually quite intelligent people. Alcoholics are found in every walk of life and roughly one out of every ten or twelve drinking people do become alcoholics. The third new learning theory I mentioned briefly before is that "never again" thing. Never again is an awfully long time for us to deal with and the program tells us (the AA program) that just for today, just for this twenty-four hour period, we will not take a drink. Will power for me, and for many others of us, was not enough. The old learning has to be changed then into new concepts because alcoholics do come to the point in their lives where they're completely unmanageable unless they intend to learn new concepts and acquire new attitudes. If this doesn't happen, then it's very likely that they will go back to either drinking or to abusing medication.

Alcoholics, again, must continually be reminded and especially by other people that they have a problem. We find our greatest help in this area by attending AA meetings. I wonder, too, how willing we are to spend a lot of time in the AA program. Many of us spent long hours drinking, twenty hours a week maybe, twenty-five hours a week. Period of time got away from us because we were drinking and forgot the long time lapses. But if we go to two or three meetings a week that would represent maybe six or nine hours depending on how long a time it took us to get to the meeting and back. So, a commitment to AA and that way of life requires at least a reasonable amount of time and as reasonable as what we spent previously on drinking.

There are a lot of cliches in AA. We hear about "Easy does it." We hear about "First things first." We hear about "A day at a time" and "Let go and let God." We do not use a lot of labels. AA has that earthy term to a dry drunk and I think the psychiatrists refer to this as a free-floating anxiety. That sounds better, more educated.

We're not looking necessarily for titles; we're looking for a way to stay sober, and the answer to that really is reinforcement. When people come out of treatment centers they could be disillusioned into the fact that there's a different world out there. But things are very much the same as when they left them. Traffic jams are just as aggravating. The kids are just as disruptive at home. If it's a wife, or a husband, or a sister, or a brother, or a colleague, they can be just as nagging as they were before. A lot of things don't change just because a person has been in and out of a treatment center. We have to know what we're going to do when we get upset by things and the question is--is that going to lead us to take a drink or not? Are we going to be discouraged and want to drink again?

There are some specific difficulties that people who come out of treatment should be aware of. One of them is job worry. (I don't know how much that would affect us.) We seek to be very fortunate in having jobs before we go into treatment and after we come out of treatment, but some people when they come out of the hospital have a worry about that. It's a good idea to have some kind of work lined up following treatment. Perhaps the job a person had was in jeopardy; perhaps he was fired. It might be necessary at this time to take a job that will not require so much time or quite so much psychic energy. We really don't experience too many financial difficulties, but it could be that we borrowed money from people and have not made any attempt to pay that money back. So, straightening up our finances is a good idea, because it's one less worry.

Then, too, I think we will be surprised, after being sober for a little bit, at how much money we can save by not spending money on booze and not spending money on pills, not spending money making unnecessary phone calls, or making purchases of things that we don't really need.

Then there are high spots that we sometimes have to be careful about. These are the prosperous times, times of success. Some alcoholics do not handle compliments too well. They're overwhelmed by them and I think a lot of us can remember that we drank in times of sadness and we drank in times of joy. That would make it just about always.

Then the dry drunk I'm going to refer to once more--the free floating anxiety is a very comfortable feeling. It happens periodically. It comes and goes and it's a kind of uncomfortable feeling. When I don't feel well physically or emotionally or spiritually I might be inclined to say to myself, "If I feel this rotten while I'm sober, maybe I would just as well off drinking."

I learned a word when I came into the program--halt. The "h" stands for hungry and the "a" for anxiety and the "l" for lonely and the "t" for tired. These are just little guidelines or little words of caution--they were a big help to me.

Another thing to be aware of is a period of delayed fatigue. Anywhere from six months to a couple of years after he stops drinking, there is a kind of natural period of delayed fatigue. I think we get very exhilarated if we're first sober and want to cure everybody in the world and save everybody. As we do this for a while our engines are inclined to run down a little bit. But with the delayed fatigue, we shouldn't be too alarmed. It's a good idea at our meetings, for instance, to talk about how we feel and to share those feelings with other people. Let them know that we are going through a period of exhaustion, that this is happening to us.

I think most of us are aware of the fact that alcoholism is a family disease. The attitude of children in the family, of family people, and the attitude of the spouse sometimes requires a lot of understanding. It does for them, and the children can get help from a group called Alateen because they're going to be very tense. The spouse or brothers and sisters can join Al-Anon; that's their type of self-help, their recovery program. I think most of us understand that the person who lives with an active alcoholic is going through an emotional alcoholism, being subjected to all kinds of worries and concerns and anxieties over the person who is drinking. So there will be a period, especially when a person first comes out of treatment, when the family will need special helps. These can be gotten through Alateen and Al-Anon.

Sometimes the person comes home from a treatment a little paranoid and suspicious. The families are too, because we know that when we're drinking we're not consistent in the things that we do. Maybe one day we're in school and the next day we're not. These are adjustments that have to be made in a reasonable length of time.

Then the new self-image has to be created. That seems always to be a big concern, perhaps not so much in community life but more in your social area. Your big concern is, "Should I tell people I don't drink anymore?" If you tell them that you don't drink anymore, they won't expect you to drink. If you don't tell them, they might be opening the door to the possibility of your taking a drink.

Then with regard to doctors--a word of caution, this has been mentioned here very often. It's the responsibility of the person who is alcoholic to let the physician know that. The thing is that an alcoholic cannot take any addictive medication. Even the labels on over the counter drugs should be checked. I'm thinking particularly of cough medicine, of sleeping pills, of bromides, or Alka-Seltzer, or mouthwash. Some of those things have a high content of alcohol and could become addictive, even some vitamins. For people who take pills, or aspirins, it's a very simple and very quick process to become addicted over them. If one pill is good we think that two or three or four would be much better.

Then the testing of ourselves. I heard a lady not too long ago say that she really tested herself when she went to a Christmas office party. She knew in her heart that she shouldn't have been there. She went and she didn't drink, but she was somewhat of a wreck by the time she got home. She declared afterward that she would never do it again. If I ever forget one minute that I'm an alcoholic, that's the exact minute that I might take a drink. What we're told in the program is to stick with winners, to get on the telephone, and talk to somebody who is in the program and to go to meetings as our reminders. AA really--and I think we're all very much aware of this, except perhaps in the beginning--is not a refuge and it's not a lonely hearts club, it's not a finance department. Some people go and look for other things besides sobriety. What it does is help us to learn to be sober.

Three big helps of staying sober are: 1. reading the right books (and I'll talk about that in a moment), 2. having a good sponsor and, 3. getting to meetings. I was told a long time ago, and I do believe it, it's much easier to stay sober once I'm sober than it is to get sober. That refers to anybody who has been sober and goes back to drinking.

I think most of you know that this is what we call the Big Book, The Alcoholics Anonymous book. To us it's comparable to our Bible and we read it cover to cover, particularly Chapter 5--How It Works. That's read at our AA meetings. We know that this book not only tells us how to get sober, but also how to stay sober. This is written through much blood and sweat and tears and we do believe that what's in it is true. The men who wrote that were winners. Then, this book Alcoholics Anonymous Comes of Age--that's also an AA publication. There's just a short excerpt that I'd like to share with you. It's Dr. Thibault's surrender process. I don't know it any of you have heard it. It was referred to last night by Rev. Penninger in his talk on surrender. I'll share just a little bit of it and you'll get an idea of where the surrender theory came from --

Finally, fortune smiled at me again. This time from another patient. For sometime she had been under my brand new (under my new brand) of psychotherapy designed to promote hitting bottom. For reasons completely unknown, she experienced a mild but typical conversion which brought her into a positive state of mind. Led by the newly found spiritual elements, she started attending various churches in town. One Monday morning she entered my office, her eyes ablaze, and at once commenced talking. "I know what happened to me. I heard it in church yesterday. I surrendered."

With the word "surrender" she handed me my first real awareness of what happens during the period of hitting bottom. The individual alcoholic was always citing an admission of being licked, of admitting that he was powerless. If and when he surrendered, he quit fighting. He admitted he was licked, and accepted the fact that he was powerless and needed help. If he did not surrender, a thousand cries could hit him and nothing constructive would happen. The need to induce surrender became a new therapeutic goal.

The miracle of AA was now a little clearer, though the reason was still obscure why the program in the fellowship of AA could induce a surrender which could in turn lead to a period of no drinking. As might be expected, I enjoyed a thrill of my own. I was getting in on what was happening--all of it an enjoyable experience. Still questioning eagerly, I shifted my therapeutic attack. The job now was to induce surrender. But I ran into a whole nest of resistances to that idea. Totally new territory had to be explored. As I continued my tour, it became ever apparent that in everyone's psyche there existed an unconquerable ego which bitterly opposed any thought of defeat. Until that ego was somehow reduced or rendered ineffective, no likelihood of surrender could be anticipated. The shift in emphasis in hitting bottom to surrender through ego reduction, occurred during the first five or six years of my initial contact with AA

So that's where the surrender process came from and that's in the book Alcoholics Anonymous Comes of Age. Another book which is recommended for reading is the twelve steps of the program and the twelve traditions of the program. These are written up in very readable fashion. It doesn't take long to read this and it'll give you a good understanding of what the members in the AA program try to practice and adhere to.

The last one of these is little twenty-four hour a day book which is offered to us in the program and it's divided up also very simply. Each day of the year is dated and at the top section is given the thought for the day. The middle section is the meditation of the day, and down at the bottom is the prayer for the day. So this is a little spiritual nosegay with which we begin our day, our twenty-four hour period where we ask for the desire to stay sober each morning.

So much for the reading because that does reinforce new learning. I don't know about some of you--as often as I read the big book or any of the AA literature, I read new things into it with each reading. There's a new approach and a fresh outlook toward it.

I think another opportunity which is very important is the taking a step forward in the program, which is writing the fearless and searching moral inventory and then, following that, the opportunity of taking the fifth step either with a clergyman or someone in the program whom I trust very much, and whose confidentiality I enjoy. This is a great spiritual boost. While we do not talk about AA being a religious program, we do know that the spiritual benefits of the program are magnificent, and that it is a miracle working program just day by day.

So, getting into AA is a tremendous reinforcement. We know that we can now substitute the AA members for the bottle. We know that the AA members are students of sobriety and always open to new and better ways of learning how to live a sober and a serene life and a sane life.

This article originally appeared in <u>*NCCA Blue Book*</u> *26 (1974): 144-152. It is reprinted with permission.*

FOURTH AND FIFTH STEPS

Rev. John P. Cunningham

*Frequently, alcoholics take their fifth
step with a priest, minister, or rabbi.
Father Cunningham offers advice as to
how the pastoral minister can effectively
"hear" a fifth step.*

Talking about the fifth step is a very difficult thing,
because many persons have in mind the question of how to
take that step. They want a sort of blueprint to follow. We
are not talking about a person's taking the fifth step for his
own personal sobriety, but rather about who is available to
receive that fifth step action from a person striving for
sobriety. I believe that availability, on my part as a member
of the program, is a serious responsibility because, if it has
to be given, it has to be taken and somebody has to be
there to take it. I firmly believe that clergy and religious
are in a particularly good position to accept the fourth and
fifth steps from the people in the program. There are many
reasons, one of them being the basic trust that people have
in clergy and religious. Most people feel that they can put
their trust in us and the confidence won't be betrayed. In
my experience in AA, too many people have trusted too
easily and some people have violated trust. I am going to
talk for a moment or two about the involvement I have had,
and what it has done for me.

During the experience of accepting the fourth and fifth
step from individuals trying to grow in spiritual life through
the AA program, believe me, I think in every instance I
have come away the winner. It's a chore, it's a difficult job,
it's a sacrifice of time and effort, and sometimes deep
emotional involvement, but on the other hand the insights
I have developed into myself in reference to my own

sobriety through being available to other people have far outweighed the convenience that we might think would be imposed upon us.

There are a lot of different factors. I've spent then years as a chaplain in the CATC, Chicago Alcoholic Treatment Center. When we opened up the center I was asked if I would do the kind of work in the fourth and fifth step that they do at the Guest House. That was exactly the way they put it, the Guest House facility. At that time, the Guest House minimal stay was four months, whereas the stay at the CATC was 21 days. There is a big difference right there. How much sobriety does a person actually gain in 21 days? In a very short time I found out that I wasn't really doing a fourth and fifth step with people in that hospital. I was only helping them deal with some very critical moral crisis in their lives at that particular moment. I could help them work through some little things that were major in their lives at that time and help them benefit a little more from the treatment, but it was in no way relating to the fourth and fifth step, the "searching and fearless moral inventory." At that time I made the judgment--I still believe it is a true judgment--that in 21 days you don't have the cobwebs clear enough to do any searching, particularly within yourself.

I also noticed something that was going on: the therapies that were going on in the hospital were also conditioning people to understand themselves better almost in the same context as the fourth and fifth step, but I developed the pattern in the hospital that when a person said fourth and fifth step, I'd say, "Let's be realistic about it. We can talk now about the moral conflicts that you have, and maybe later on we can get together, and when you've developed a little more sobriety, have a little more time, when you've got a better understanding and appreciation of the first three steps we will better understand why you want to do it. I don't really think that it is a setting in which fourth and fifth steps, as such, can be done.

Guilt and the Moral Conflict

However, I think in that setting there has to be some kind of dealing with the moral conflicts that a person takes into treatment. Everybody here who has gone into AA or gone into treatment facilities knows the guilt factor that was present in the beginning of your recovery process, and it is not something that can be dealt with in a very brief span of time.

I've also been involved in retreat work; I have averaged about four or five retreats a year through the last 25 or 26 years and that's a lot of retreats. A lot of people come ready to make the fourth and fifth steps in the retreat setting. If I am going to do justice to some 50 or 60 people, I always found it rather difficult to really deal with anybody in the depth that seems to me to be required for the fourth and fifth step action in the AA program. My reply usually is, "All right, if you have something specific you want to deal with at this time, we can deal with it right here and right now," and then I would make arrangements; usually they are people from the area in which I live; that's where I usually give retreats although I do branch out to other places. I make arrangements for them to come out and see me at the office where we can go at it a little bit more in depth. If it is a person from out of town, I would tell them, "We'll deal with some of the things you feel are significant right now but I would recommend very highly that you would find somebody in your home area that would be helpful in taking you through these very critical steps of the program." My main experience in this particular area is not so much from an institutional setting, as it is from a pastoral setting, an I'll just bring into focus a few conclusions that I have in my own mind, a few judgments that I have made, on taking the fourth and fifth step in the pastoral setting.

The first one is the major one. All alcoholics are not alike and I think that you cannot draw a blueprint of what is exactly your role in guiding a person through this particular phase of his recovery program. Let's mention some differences. I've gone through the fourth and fifth steps with people whose drinking careers lasted two years. In those two years they only saw themselves as becoming alcoholics. They were actually alcoholics; the evidences were there, but they didn't get into the deep real hard deterioration that would go with the maybe twenty or thirty years of constant alcoholic drinking and so you wouldn't deal in the fourth and fifth step level with those people in exactly the same way.

Secondly, back when I started working with the fourth and fifth step the number of treatment facilities that were available were very, very few but now you have treatment facilities available all over. When we speak of treatment facilities I think there is a major kind of facility that we don't frequently enough consider and that is counseling services. The number of people who go through counseling services in relation to their alcohol or drug problems also are a factor in what goes on in these fourth and fifth steps. If you are looking for a blueprint on how to involve yourself in it, I think you would have to say, "Forget it; there is not blueprint." I think that Carl Rogers in his later days as a clinical psychologist came to the conclusion that counselling is not really an act at all; it's a relationship and that's about the way I go in the present time.

I'll tell you some of the first steps that I go through. If a person comes and says, "Can I do my fourth and fifth steps with you?" I say, "Yes," tentatively, and I say "Will you come in and we'll talk about it?" One of the reasons why I don't do a total commitment to it is that I really don't know how I am going to relate to this particular individual. What I am saying, I guess, is, "Maybe I am not the person for you. I would like to find that out, and I would like you to find that out, too."

Look for the Motives

One of the first questions I ask when people come in is, "Why do you want to take that fourth and fifth steps?" I have found many people who are not very well motivated for going through this particular stage of their recovery program. I frequently enough get people who will say, "Well it's on the card," or words to that effect. I think that reflects the idea that they are doing a scientific exercise, a lesson plan type thing. A "I have to do the fourth step today and fifth step tomorrow thing," and I don't think that's really an adequate thing. So we inquire into motivation and maybe I'll spend a whole session helping the person to develop some good reasons why.

Another thing in the first session that I try to get is a whole good background; married, single, man, woman, all those kinds of factors that are significant. I really feel that I have to know the individual a great deal more before I can actually figure out what later on they might be telling me, how it fits into the total scheme of their life, because I feel again that the fourth and fifth steps should be a moral inventory of our lives, not just of our drinking career, but of our lives, and I think that I have to know something about their lives. Usually, I spend that initial session in getting to know the person fairly well so that when they do talk about things and present the actual development of their fifth step revelation I can know what the context is, not just the text alone.

Now I'll talk from my own experience for a few moments, how I did it in my own life. I made about ten false starts. I was sober about four or five months. I said, "I am ready for the fourth and fifth steps," and I did it, after the manner of the old fashioned confession, "Bless me Father for I have sinned; I did this six times, this eight times and this 29 times, and forgive me." It was getting into details. I was ignorant at that particular phase of my life. For instance I actually sat in a meeting one time and I said, "I never had resentments in my life, I only hate that guy's guts but I never resented anybody." I didn't know what resentment was. I made about eight or ten false starts before I actually did get a good idea of what I myself wanted to do, so that's one of the reasons why I try to help people to motivate themselves for something worthwhile. I had a particular aversion to the old Hazelden <u>Guide to the Twelve Step Inventory</u> because to me it was very, very scientific. The new one is far better because they try to get into the personal dynamics rather than the scientific theological things and the personal dynamics is far more important. I think that in speaking of a moral inventory we can't ignore the Ten Commandments, but I don't think that the impact of the inventory is personal morality. I inquire into a personal morality and see how these particular things that they are revealing are offensive to this person. How am I offending myself in the things that I am trying to reveal through the fourth and fifth steps? Now as far as the amount of time spent, I've gone as many as twelve sessions with people who wanted to do their fifth step. I've gone as many as one, or as few as one, because some people come in, they haven't been hurt that much, and they haven't got themselves deeply involved in a deterioration, and so they don't have an awful lot to reflect.

Take the Steps in Order

And then a final observation is this. I think that when I am doing the fourth and fifth step with an individual I am highly conscious of the third step. The way I look at it the first three steps are the beginning of the program and then that third step says we made a decision to turn our lives and our wills over to the care of God as we understood him. The question that comes to my mind is what life, what will and that's where your answer begins in the fourth and fifth steps. This is my life and this is my will. This is the way it works with me and what do I have to straighten out here and then I don't think you can isolate that fourth and fifth step, either, from the sixth and seventh. "Became entirely ready," so I think you are looking back to discover what kind of life and will I am turning over to God's care, and you are looking ahead to helping this person come to some conclusions and decisions about what are some of the things that I am going to change. Now I don't want to go into any kind of details at all about the kinds of things that you are going to hear in the fourth and fifth step, or how you are going to deal with them. In this setting that's not appropriate. In the setting of a fourth and fifth step, that's the guts of it; that's the most important thing. But everybody has his own life, and everybody is affected in his own life by the consequences of guilt. They are all affected by the denial syndrome in their own lives, and so these are some of the things that have to be dealt with, but it's so different with everybody that you are dealing with that you can't do a blueprint.

I think that, in conclusion, I would say this: First of all, don't look for a blueprint; there isn't any. This person is the one I am working with, and he's entirely unique and separate from everybody else. The second conclusion: don't try to set a time framework. Don't put yourself in a time framework because I think sometimes I have been unjust trying to help these people do it in one sitting and knowing very well that there were a lot of questions left unasked, and a lot of answers left unexplored. I don't accept somebody coming in and sitting down for an hour and saying, "All right, I'm through. Now I can be happy forevermore." It doesn't exactly work that way. It's a relationship that we enter into and I think that we have to commit ourselves to more in terms of time, and a great deal more in terms of personal morality than in terms of theoretical or theological morality.

This article originally appeared in <u>NCCA Blue Book</u> 30 (1978): 268-272. It is reprinted with permission.

WHY CALIX....OUR MEMBERS TELL US

Gene Trow

Calix is an organization of Catholics who have recovered through AA It grew from a group of alcoholics wishing to fully live AA's eleventh step in their lives.

Quite frequently, as I have discussed Calix with Catholic newcomers in AA and the added spiritual benefits available in the Calix Society for the problem Catholic drinker, I am confronted with the very normal and logical question: Why Calix?

The answer is found in the Eleventh Step of the Alcoholics Anonymous program, "We sought through prayer and meditation to improve our conscious contact with God, **as we understood Him**, praying only for the knowledge of His will for us, and the power to carry it out."

How does the Catholic problem drinker understand God? Following this admonition by AA, I submit to you that we understand Him first at the knee of our mother as a child, learning the simple, formal prayers of the church, later by the teaching of the good nuns or priests, and finally participating in the sacramental life of the church. That is exactly the reasoning and interpretation of the founders of our Calix Society. It is simple as that.

I firmly believe that our quest for serenity lies in the restoration of our friendship with God, as we understand Him. I believe St. Augustine, one of the great saints of Christendom, expressed this thought in a most beautiful way after his conversion from a life of bitter turmoil; "Our hearts will never rest, oh Christ, until they rest in Thee". Isn't this true of each of us who knows so well the agonizing days of our alcoholic affliction? Pray God that we reach out for this added dimension in our spiritual rehabilitation to fortify ourselves against an illness that gives no quarter.

This article originally appeared in <u>Chalice</u> 10.2 (1984): 4. It is reprinted with permission.

HITTING THE KNEEL ON THE HEAD

Rabbi Samuel A. Rothberg

What works for one individual does not always work for another. In giving guidance, pastoral ministers need to consider the alcoholic's spiritual background.

At AA, Al-Anon and other self-help meetings many participants talk about the practice of praying in a kneeling position. Occasionally I'm asked about this by recovering Jewish substance abusers. They often express a certain discomfort with this unfamiliar prayer posture. I would like to share this Hasidic parable about the proper posture for prayer.

"The Hasidic rabbi, Menahem Mendel of Premislan, once declared three things are fitting for us: kneeling upright, motionless dancing and silent screaming. Kneeling is not only a matter of physical posture, it can also be a spiritual attitude. Thus we can kneel even when we are upright. A man can stand erect and feel humility and reverence in his heart. Dancing is not only a matter of outward movement, it can also be an inner mood. We can dance motionless. Prayer is not always articulate, often it is unspoken yearning alone. We can cry out silently."

Perhaps this parable will serve as a guide for those who are concerned about kneeling in prayer.

This article originally appeared in JACS Journal 3.2 (1986): 7. It is reprinted with permission.

A DIALOGUE: SCRIPTURE AND THE ADULT CHILDREN OF ALCOHOLICS

Sister Rea McDonnell, S.S.N.D.

Adult children of alcoholics have suffered as a result of their parent's alcoholism. Scripture can help these adult children develop serenity.

It crops up everywhere. People are talking about, writing about adult children of alcoholics. As a spiritual director and teacher in renewal programs for religious and priests, I too have heard many variations on the theme. Let me relate how one woman's experience of healing began.

Sister Linda had set aside a day for prayer as Holy Week approached. Fifteen years professed, 35 years old, she was successful in community, ministry, and prayer. She especially enjoyed Ignatian contemplation, using her imagination to see gospel scenes in technicolor. As she prayed with the passion account, she visualized Jesus trudging under the weight of his cross. Suddenly, more than her imagination operated; this scene "seized" her--Jesus' friend John ran alongside Jesus, skirting the crowds that lined the way to Calvary. Linda heard his frantic cries, "Jesus, don't do this! Don't go through with it! Why are you doing this?"

Jesus looked at his friend and replied, "I'm doing this for Linda." "That slut," John retorted. "She is not a slut!" Jesus drew himself up straight and enunciated each word as if his whole life were in it (and it was). "She is not a slut. She is mine." Linda's very secret wound--her alcoholic mother's constant and vicious disapproval of her--began its long process of healing.

Many adult children of alcoholics in religious communities can tell of similar moments in prayer or in friendship, at an Al-Anon meeting or now, at the newly forming Adult Children of Alcoholics (ACA) meetings. In my ministry of spiritual direction I am amazed at how many women and men religious are indeed the adult children of alcoholics, amazed at how that has shaped their lives, and how structures of grace and health gradually replace the unhealthy family structures.

In this article I hope to put some pieces of scripture into dialogue with the experience of being an adult child of an alcoholic. In three sections I will treat of three unspoken warnings to the child in an alcoholic family: don't trust, don't feel, don't talk. How do these three core experiences block prayer, that is, relationship with God? More importantly, what is the grace inherent in those three attitudes once the Word of God can begin to liberate?

There are many theories of what causes compulsive behavior. Inconsistency in the family of origin is one I learned of long ago. The adult children of alcoholics are compulsive; no wonder, when the overarching experience in the alcoholic family is inconsistency--not just inconsistent pay checks or meals but inconsistent, sometimes all or nothing, affection, approval, presence. The compulsive person may grow into adulthood addicted to tidiness or punctuality, to purity or scrimping, to hard work or sickness or silence. Some of these behaviors were rewarded in pre-Vatican religious life. Religious who could not trust in relationships were reinforced by warnings about particular friendships; those who could not feel were called sweet and obedient; those who could not talk about anything of significance were "contemplative." Some of us, for all the compulsiveness of our "striving for perfection" truly were obedient and contemplative. Although we thought we were leaving the inconsistencies of home behind when we entered the novitiate, we carried the results, our own addictions, non-alcoholic though they might be, into our religious congregations. There, however, the Word of God, like snow or rain, could begin to penetrate the earth.

If scripture had to be distilled into just one theme, it might be freedom: Israel's and our own freedom from slavery into exodus toward a new and trusted promise, a covenant; Jesus' and our freedom from fear through rejection, abandonment, and pain to new life. If all the images and qualities of God in scripture had to be distilled, we would know that God's love is unconditional (hesed) and consistent, faithful (emet), and made very tangible in Jesus. The ultimate gift of God to each of us, good or bad, manipulative or surrendering, chaste or unchaste, obedient or disobedient, kind or gruff, is freedom. Sometimes we name that freedom, Spirit.

Don't Trust

The trust of babies, toddlers, and teenagers in their alcoholic parents seesaws. Now tended and petted and rocked, then ignored and hungry and chaffed, babies in alcoholic families begin life never quite negotiating the primary task which Erik Erickson terms basic trust. No wonder the self-image of adult children is fragile; no wonder adult children are moody and possessive. Moods, modeled on their parents, shift erratically. Comfort must be possessed and clung to. These children may especially cling to those who provide comfort: superiors, friends, spiritual directors; or they may cling to comforts of prestige, sleep, chocolate, work.

With such troubled parents, their children may find that God imagined as either father or mother is inadequate, even painful. To replace "father" with "mother" will still disappoint. Both parents, even a non-drinking parent, are involved with alcohol. Thus the "good" parent, the long-suffering provider of care, must be demythologized, painfully taken down from the ACA pedestal. Gradually the ACA has to see how addicted to alcohol the "good" parent was too, how the children might be neglected while the co-dependent (even though non-drinking) would give the spouse every attention while the alcoholic was drinking, every affection when the alcoholic was trying to quit. Often the ACA have only co-dependent parents are models of loving--and such models can have many unhealthy aspects.

Our scriptures offer us hundreds of images of God. We need not be limited to parental images. God is so much more than father or mother. I invite readers to find five or ten images of God in scripture. I invite them to make up their own. Slowly, over a period of time, pray through the 50 psalms to find praise of God's **hesed** and **emet**, translated as "faithful love" or "mercy endures forever" or "everlasting kindness." In the New Testament, too, we have a marvelous model of loving in Jesus' loving. Move slowly through a gospel (Mark's or Luke's would be best) to observe Jesus' love: tender, tough, blessing, blaming, eager, angry. It is a love to be counted on, no matter how inadequate (Peter), inauthentic (Zacchaeus), slutty (the weeping woman in Luke 7), controlling (Martha), or lost (Mary in John 11) one feels. It is a love to be trusted.

In my work with directees I find that many of them seek peace in prayer. Of course, I hope that eventually they want God, not peace. No wonder peace is often equated with God. In the turbulence of family life, visits, novenas, bedside prayers were means of comfort for the children. When God does not produce peace for them as adults, they feel abandoned. Ours is an urge to control prayer and our relationship with God, even God's own self--the one who is ultimately free. If we discover that we cannot control God, it is no wonder that we try to control and cling to every satisfying human relationship. Both separation and surprises seem more painful for the ACA.

Continued praying with images of God's hesed and emet, with eyes fixed on Jesus, with looking for God in daily dyings and risings, and remembering God's kindness concretely in specific past events may all help an ACA to be more receptive to what is, after all, God's gift of trust. Inviting Jesus into a painful memory of childhood, listening to him take charge of the situation when we were so helpless and hurt, is another helpful prayer exercise.[1]

Don't Feel

The family of alcoholics also picks up denial as a defense--especially defense of painful reality. The family denies truth, the truth of the alcoholic's disease, the emotional desertion conflicts which might spring up but which are quickly suppressed in hopelessness. Members of the family learn to "control," to deny their true feelings. As the ACA begins to heal, feelings become an important locus of grace, God's own life within. A long process is needed for ACA's, to pray daily to the Spirit of truth not to deny reality. The rigid roles played in the family begin to shift as freedom happens. It seems that certain roles lead to certain denials and certain graces.

Particularly the "family hero" denies fear. Heroes have to be strong and brave so that younger siblings, perhaps even co-dependent parents, can depend on them. Heroes can translate childhood stability, generosity, sense of

---

[1]Dennis and Matthew Linn, S.J., **Healing Life's Hurts** (Ramsey, N.J.: Paulist Press, 1976).

responsibility into adult ministries of foreign missions, leadership, or, simply, messiah. In its worst form, heroes build empires, and in that self-deception common to the alcoholic family, name it self-sacrifice for God's kingdom. Jesus was not a workaholic. He was free. Religious whose unflagging energy never quits can be repeating unhealthy patterns of denying loneliness or fear learned at home. The Spirit of truth can set them free from compulsions, from needing to be brave and strong, from needing to save the world.

The "lost child" tends to be passive. Such "docile" behavior was once rewarded. On the other hand, freely receiving from God and others is an antidote to much that is macho in our culture. The attitude lost children need to pray for is gratitude, for they know in their bones, from their former family life, that everything now of joy and peace and love is gift. They also, however, need to focus on anger in prayer--that of God, of Jesus, or their own, both past and present. Because they have volcanos of rage within them and are so afraid of eruptions, they may need counseling in conjunction with direction in order to explore their anger.

The "mascot" denies sadness and despair, and often, in denying all feelings, seems superficial. If set free by truth, he/she can use the practiced wit and charm to communicate joy. One directee who had been praying the "don't let me deny" prayer for two years finally felt ready to cry. Her charm and her cheer were not holding. She continued with me but entered therapy too for she said she might drown in all her years of tears, and at least a therapist would know how to swim.

Psalms are particularly helpful to those who are ashamed to feel. Patterns of Prayer in the Psalms by Laurence

Dunlop [2]treats very well how cursing, crying, and laying it all out before God, to God, are to be done. Lament derives from the Hebrew word **lamah** (why), the "Why?" of the fearful, angry, sorrowful Job, Jeremiah, and Jesus. When someone feels blocked emotionally in prayer, a return to the psalms is helpful to get the juices flowing again.

Jesus' feelings are the centerpiece of Catholic psychologist Andrew Canale's excellent paperback, Understanding the Human Jesus. [3] The humanity of Jesus also gives us permission to be human. He is like us in everything, in every single emotion we have ever dared to feel. Jesus felt them all, did not deny any of them, then used them or let them go. Sometimes he was in control of his feelings, but sometimes (raging in the temple, sweating fear and blood, cursing a fig tree, and insulting his friend Peter) they were in control of him. He could risk letting his feelings control him because he knew that God's gifts of emotions, of feeling everything, are good.

Feelings might provide the religious who are "striving for perfection" the most difficulty. Perfection often meant control not only of our behavior but even our feelings which were equated with behavior. Matthew offers us the ideal: "Be perfect as your heavenly father is perfect." In Greek "perfect" simply means headed toward the goal; surely the goal is God, not emotional control. Luke however encourages us to deep and long-lasting emotions which

---

2   Laurence Dunlop, Patterns of Prayers in the Psalms (New York: Seabury Press, Inc., 1982).

3   Andrew Canale, Understanding the Human Jesus (Ramsey, N.J.: Paulist Press, 1985).

Aquinas named passions. Luke 6:36 exhorts: "Be compassionate as your father is compassionate" i.e., **compassion:** share the very passions of God. ACA need to feel the passion, acknowledge it as God's gift to Jesus and to us, then decide whether to use it channeled as **compassion** or let it go. That decision is best made not in compulsive fear or in the name of "perfection" but in freedom.

Don't Talk

Growing up with alcoholic parents is usually as closely guarded a secret in religious life as one's sex or prayer life. This is **the** family secret. Religious in their 40's and 50's assure me that I am the first person ever to hear their guilty shame. Sometimes they believe that they are responsible for the drinking of their parent(s). Intelligent medical people tell me alcoholism is a disease--in every other family but their own.

"Don't talk" flies in the face of perhaps the most joyful of all religious doctrines: God's word, so creative, powerful, saving; God's word became flesh. We hear God's word in scripture, the ups and downs of daily living, the affirmations and challenges of human relationships and especially in Jesus, alive and with us, within us. Ours is a religion of the Word, our faith an adherence, a clinging only to the Word who is Christ. "If you make my word your home," with which Jesus prefaces his famous promise: "You will know the truth and the truth will set you free" (Jn 8:32). The home life which needs so much healing is invited into the word. There is nothing we can do to change our alcoholic parent(s) or transform the co-dependency of the other parent, although many ACA who are religious keep trying. Instead, the word offers them a new home, a dwelling place.

The word of God, of Jesus, is true. Just as the word spoken through the prophets consoled and critiqued, so this word will not just be a cozy, warm word/home. The word will call for discipline, disciple-making activity. **Discipulus/a** means learner in Latin. "If you make my word your home, you will be my disciples, you will know the truth and the truth will set you free." This word will call for conflict. [4]

One cannot control the word of God (Is 55). In religious life of the past, our words were controlled by bells and great silence. Now I find the outpouring of words to be an effective form of denial. Directees who hardly stop for breath are hurting, covering the true word with a bevy of words. When asked: "What hurts?" their eyes pop open. ACA need to be cared for. No one asked them as they were growing up, beyond the skinned knee or football accident, what hurts? They may be frightened to put their pain into words for the words create pain, fear, and fury. Laying open the wounds in prayer, telling or at least showing the wounds to Jesus, asking him to "kiss them and make them better" may be the child-like start of healing.

Talking may begin the remedy. The risk is not to deny the truth but to say it: to oneself, to God, eventually to another. Trusting and feeling will probably tag along. Facing truth may come through a religious experience like Sister Linda's--she who had never made reference to her mother's disease in prayer (God, after all, had never answered her childhood prayer that her mother stop drinking). It may come from risking a word of truth to a

---

[4] I recommend, particularly on the topics of communication and conflict, Fran Ferder, Word Made Flesh (Notre Dame: Ave Maria Press, 1986).

friend. It may arise from a friend's or spiritual director's direct question. The truth may be exposed to a counselor or a therapist. Group spiritual direction with other ACA could be particularly helpful.

The past life of ACA--ourselves, our friends, those we direct--is terribly wounded. The image I would leave us with is Jesus on Easter night. He returned to the very friends who had abandoned him, proclaiming peace to them, and showing them his wounds--not repressed, suppressed, denied, or unfelt wounds. They were real wounds, scars of suffering, fear and abandonment both by friends and by God--but now, glorified wounds. Jesus could not undo the horror of a Good Friday any more than the ACA can undo a past of pain. In laying the pain and fear and feelings before God, however, like Jesus we can be healed and immersed in new life, life in abundance.

This article originally appeared in Sisters Today *(February, 1987) and is reprinted with permission of the author.*

For Further Reading on
Spiritual Issues in Recovery

Arms, M. (1984). Priest Lays to Rest 5th Step Obstacles. Chalice, 10(1), 5.

In this article, Fr. Arms "tries to show some of the obstacles [of taking step 5] and, at the same time, tried to lay to rest those obstacles."

Berenson, D. (July/August 1987). Alcoholics Anonymous: From Surrender to Transformation. Networker, 25-31.

In this study of AA, Berenson emphasizes the conversion experience in recovery.

Bill W. (1988). The Language of the Heart. New York: AA Grapevine.

The book is a selection of Grapevine articles written by AA's co-founder which cover various aspects of the AA program.

Campbell, C. (December 1988). Spirituality and the AA Movement. Priest, 12-14.

This article is the text for a talk that Bishop Campbell delivered at the 1988 North American AA convention. He argues "that the work of the AA movement and the work of the Church are beautiful compliments to one another."

Christian, M. (1983). Turning It Over. In J. Swallow (ed.), Out From Under. (pp. 50-51). San Francisco: Spinsters Ink.

Christian, a recovered lesbian alcoholic, includes the words and music for a song she wrote about AA's third step.

Conroy, W. J. (September 1988). Calix: A Program for Catholic Alcoholics. Ligourian, 42-43.

134

Conroy explains the work of Calix, a society of Roman Catholics who recovered in AA

Cox, W. F. (1983). A Spiritual Foundation. Alcoholism. (pp. 287-291). Lancaster: M & P Press, Ltd.

Cox describes the spiritual foundation of AA.

Crosby, L. R., & Bissell, L. (1989). To Care Enough: Intervention with Chemically Dependent Colleagues -- A Guide for Healthcare and Other Professionals. Minneapolis, Minnesota: Johnson Institute Book.

Although the focus of this book is on working with health care professionals, the material presented is valuable for those wishing to do an intervention with an alcoholic priest, nun, or religious brother.

DeKruif, P. H. (1960). How Faith Helps to Cure Alcoholism. Today's Health, 38(4), 61-63.

The "higher power" in AA is emphasized in this article which summarizes AA philosophy and the organization's origins.

Donnelly, P. (1974). The Experience of Spiritual Recovery. NCCA Blue Book, 36, 180-192.

Donnelly addresses the religious nature of AA. Focus is on gratitude and the role of a higher power in the alcoholics life.

Ernie K. (1984). Ninety Meetings, Ninety Days: A Journal of Experience, Strength, and Hope. Minneapolis: Johnson Institute.

Ernie reflects on each of ninety AA meetings he attended during a ninety day period. He comments on various AA topics, steps, slogans, and readings.

Father Mac (1984). Father Mac Discusses the Twelve Steps. Milwaukee: Milwaukee AA Central Office.

Fr. Mac explains each of the 12 steps of AA.

Fichter, J. (1976). Parallel Conversions: Charismatics and Recovered Alcoholics. Christian Century, 93(5), 148-150.

Fichter delineates the similarities between an evangelical Christian conversion and the conversion experience of AA-alcoholics.

Glass, C. (1985). The Twelve Steps and the Jewish Tradition. JACS Journal, 2(1), 6-8,12.

Rabbi Glass explains how AA's twelve steps are consistent with Jewish theology.

Kurtz, E. (1989). 'Spiritual Rather Than Religious': The Contribution of Alcoholics Anonymous. in R. B. Waahlberg (ed.), Prevention and Control/Realities and Aspirations: Volume II. (pp. 678-686). Norway: National Directorate for the Prevention of Alcohol and Drug Problems.

The essay examines nine topics that support AA's claim that it is spiritual and not religious. These issues are explained in their historic context.

Luger, A. E. Calix and the Twelve Steps. Minneapolis: The Calix Society.

This book provides a Catholic interpretation of AA's twelve steps.

Mowrer, O. H. (1964). Alcoholics Anonymous and the 'Third' Reformation. Religion in Life, (34), 383-397.

Mowrer describes the ecumenical character of AA.

Christianity is seen as the first reformation, the Protestant reformation of the sixteenth-century is seen as the second, and AA is the third-- even though it doesn't consider itself a religion. Brief mention is made of "a young minister" who had asked "for advice and help in starting some AA-like groups in his church."

Nace, R. K. (1949). Alcoholics Anonymous Speaks to the Church. Journal of Clinical Pastoral Work, 2, 124-132.

Nace concludes that AA has "found a way to bring the gospel of Christ to a particular group in a successful way; and that examination of this way serves to re-emphasize the validity of the central teaching of the Church."

Peale, N. V. (April, 1989). Twelve Tremendous Steps That Will Work for Anyone. Guideposts, 2-5.

Peale interprets the twelve steps from a Christian perspective and shows how they can be used for problems other than alcohol.

Pittman, B. (1988). Stepping Stones to Recovery: Selected Spiritual Insights into Recovery Drawn from the Membership of Alcoholics Anonymous Over the Past 50 Years. Seattle, Washington: Glen Abbey Books.

Pittman's anthology includes essays of historical importance, on prayer, on meditation, on general spiritual issues, and on acceptance. It is an excellent collection of writings on AA spirituality.

Reardon, H. (1988). Sobriety and Spirituality. Chalice, 14(1), 3.

Reardon describes the differences between Calix and AA.

Reverend Jack S. (1985). Spiritual Reflections for the Recovering Alcoholic. Staten Island, New York: Alba House.

The book is a series of brief meditations on both spiritual and secular topics.

Sellner, E. C. (1981). Christian Ministry and the Fifth Step. Center City: Hazelden.

Sellner writes that "this booklet is written for Christian ministers who want to know more about AA's Fifth Step and the ministry of reconciliation associated with it."

Shoemaker, S. (1967). What the Church Has to Learn from Alcoholics Anonymous. In S. Shoemaker, And Thy Neighbor. (pp. 23- 35). Waco, TX: Word Books.

Although it is not a religious organization, Shoemaker argues that AA exemplifies lived Christianity.

Smith, R. (1976). Alcohol and Spiritual Collapse. NCCA Blue Book, 28, 74-90.

Smith explains how AA's twelve steps help the alcoholic move closer to God.

Steinman, D. (Winter 1984). Judaism and the Twelve Steps. JACS Journal, 6.

Rabbi Steinman argues that "while the Steps are not derived from Jewish sources, they do parallel basic Jewish concepts."

(1952). Twelve Steps and Twelve Traditions. New York, New York: Alcoholics Anonymous World Services, Inc.

This book explains each of AA's twelve steps and twelve traditions in detail. It is one of the basic texts used by AA alcoholics.

(1988). The Twelve Steps for Christians. San Diego, California:

Recovery Press.

The book explains how the twelve steps developed by AA and interprets them from a Christian perspective. The focus of the book is on adult children of alcoholics. Each step is individually explained.

Weinberg, J. R. (1975). <u>AA: An Interpretation for the Nonbeliever</u>. Center City, MN: Hazelden.

Weinberg interprets each of the twelve steps from the point of view of the non-believer. Several criticisms of AA are also addressed.

MINISTRY TO ALCOHOLICS
AND THEIR FAMILIES

PASTORAL CARE OF
THE CHEMICALLY DEPENDENT

Gerald B. Dooher, Ph.D.

What is the pastoral minister to do when confronted with an alcoholic? And what resources are available to help? Dr. Dooher addresses these questions in this essay.

No one can remain in pastoral ministry for very long before encountering the disease of chemical dependency and the destructive effects it has upon the lives of those it afflicts. The impact of alcoholism and other forms of chemical dependency will confront the pastoral minister more frequently and more rigorously than any other human problem. This article is intended to give pastoral ministers some practical guidelines for recognizing and ameliorating the effects of the disease.

Alcoholism is the most common form of chemical dependency. The National Council on Alcoholism reports that the direct effects of alcohol abuse account for approximately 50 percent of all hospital admissions, 25 percent of suicides, and 70 percent to 85 percent of homicides. Statistics for other forms of chemical dependency are similarly alarming.

Spouses, parents, and friends also experience difficulties because of their relationships with chemically dependent persons. These people are called **codependent**, and the unique relationship that develops between codependents and dependents is called **codependency**. These terms refer to individuals who attempt to control, change, or cure the destructive behavior of the chemically dependent person. Because of frustration in their efforts, codependent persons can experience painful feelings of anger, failure, and lowered self-esteem. Codependent people may in the long run experience medical problems such as hypertension, ulcers, or other stress-related disorders. In severe cases, codependency becomes a disease in its own right.

In parish ministry, chemical dependency and codependency usually show up within the context of chronic family conflict. Recent research findings indicate that chemical dependency exists in more than one half of troubled marriages that end in divorce. Furthermore, susceptibility to chemical dependency can be inherited. Thus, the disease is four to five times more likely to develop in children with one or two chemically dependent parents than in children of non-chemically dependent parents. Even if such children have escaped chemical dependency, they may have sustained scars that interfere with their ability to establish and maintain satisfying interpersonal relationships.

CAUTION TO MINISTERS

Men and women in pastoral ministry can become frustrated when they encounter resistance or hostility from the very people they are attempting to help. One can resist the temptation to rescue or save the chemically dependent individual, however, and focus on offering assistance based on intervention and support. It is useful to remember that to recover from the disease, each chemically dependent person must begin by taking critical steps that lead to (1) acceptance of the disease, (2) surrender to the need for help, and (3) hope that pain will subside when drug use ends.

Most chemically dependent people experience considerable shame, guilt, denial, and ignorance concerning the impact of their disease both on themselves and on the people around them. When they do seek pastoral care for the first time, they may come not out of a sense of personal need, but as angry, bewildered, or otherwise poorly motivated participants in a family's cry for help. In these cases, before treatment can be considered, the nature of the problem must be identified. Equally important, the chemically dependent person who is ignorant of or denying his or her condition must be confronted with the facts of the disease. Identification, confrontation, and referral constitute the principal tools of pastoral ministry in assisting the chemically dependent to receive treatment.

IDENTIFYING THE PROBLEM

Pastoral ministers, since they lack formal medical and psychiatric training, often feel inadequate when it comes to diagnosing chemical dependency, but they frequently do possess sufficient practical knowledge and experience to identify disease symptoms. The chief signs of dependency include those that reveal clear-cut changes in behavior and personality.

Most addictive drugs function either as depressants of brain activity or as stimulants; they are taken because of either their sedative or their euphoria-inducing properties. Examples of depressants include alcohol, minor tranquilizers, sleeping pills, and antianxiety drugs. The stimulants, such as cocaine and amphetamine ("speed"), accelerate brain activity and bodily functioning.

When a drug wears off, brain cells react to the stress of chronic drug use, and side effects result. These changes are responses to chemical "withdrawal" and can produce sensations that are opposite to those the drug user wanted to achieve. For example, when the sedative effect of alcohol or other depressant fades, anxiety, irritability, and other symptoms of nervous distress occur. Severe reactions include insomnia, panic attacks, paranoia, and in extreme cases, hallucinations and convulsions. Withdrawal from stimulants such as cocaine or amphetamine typically produces lethargy, melancholy, and depression, which can reach suicidal intensity.

For most people, the complications of withdrawal provide an effective deterrent to overindulgence, but for the chemically dependent, withdrawal fails to discourage drug abuse.

MORE DRUG NEEDED

Because chronic drug usage damages the nerve cells of the brain, the capacity to experience the desirable effects of drugs diminishes with time and continued usage. As a result, the chemically dependent person may need increasingly larger and more frequent doses to achieve intoxication and to prevent withdrawal. These changes reflect an alteration in an individual's tolerance for the drug and represent an important stage in the establishment of physical dependency. Eventually, even very large quantities of drug may fail to elicit pleasurable sensations.

These physiological and behavioral changes produce the addictive pattern of drug usage that includes three essential features: (a) compulsive drug use, (b) loss of control over the use of the drugs, and (c) continued use despite adverse consequences. Together, these three features constitute the behavioral hallmarks of chemical dependency. When this addictive stage of the disease has been reached, voluntary continuation of drug use no longer remains the choice of the chemically dependent person.

As the disease progresses, drugs produce direct effects on the brain that also bring about changes in personality and behavior. These effects can include episodes of guilt, fear, loneliness, anxiety, depression, loss of self-confidence, and lowered self-esteem, which seem to be unrelated to external circumstances. Typical self-protective behavior may include denial of the disease or its negative effects, rationalization of behavior, and withdrawal from social contacts to minimize risk of discovery. Some chemically dependent people spend years in psychotherapy or are treated in mental hospitals because the symptoms of their disease are misdiagnosed as psychiatric disorders.

Most chemically dependent people experience a decline of spiritual values as a result of their disease. For people in religious life, symptoms of chemical dependency often include dwindling involvement with vocation and disillusionment with spiritual activities. Responding to these changes, some religious choose to abandon their vocation in favor of secular life. Perhaps more frequently, the chemically dependent religious continues in ministry, but with gradually diminishing commitment and effectiveness.

CONFRONTATION IS REQUIRED

Because chemical dependency interferes with one's ability to evaluate and remedy problems, many victims of the disease must be confronted directly with evidence of their condition before they can understand the need for treatment.

The word "confrontation" has an ominous connotation for many people who understand its use in some forms of specialized, hard-hitting psychotherapy. Within the context of this article, confrontation means education and explanation.

Confrontative factual evidence, offered in an objective, nonjudgmental manner, counteracts the psychological defenses of denial, blaming, rationalization, and withdrawal, which block chemically dependent people from accepting the disease. Furthermore, knowledge of the disease's effects dispels much of their confusion, guilt, and ignorance. Often, learning about the influence of mood changers on personality, feelings, and outlook provides people with their first plausible explanation for their chronic difficulties. The chemically dependent person is then ready for further professional evaluation and treatment.

Providing a chemically dependent individual with a referral for treatment can be a more or less complicated procedure, depending on the readiness of the affected person to accept professional aid. Fortunately, dependable referral agencies, such as the National Council on Alcoholism, are available to provide recommendations based on each individual's needs. These agencies, along with physicians and substance-abuse counselors, accept the responsibility for providing referrals. Pastoral ministers can prepare to provide invaluable preliminary advice if they become acquainted with the referral agencies and treatment centers available in their area.

TREATMENT PROGRAMS ABOUND

In most parts of the United States, chemically dependent people will be able to select from a variety of different treatment options. A brief summary follows of six major types of treatment programs that may be available.

1. **Twelve Step Programs.** Some of the most successful organizations are the self-help groups based on the twelve-step program developed by Alcoholics Anonymous (AA). Similar groups include Narcotics Anonymous, Cocaine Anonymous, and Pills Anonymous. Alcoholics Anonymous is the largest of these organizations, holding weekly meetings

in large urban areas and on a more limited but regular basis in less populous settings.

Twelve-step programs provide recovering people with practical guidelines for maintaining abstinence and offer an effective approach for achieving emotional and spiritual health. If pastoral ministers were to offer no more assistance than to underscore the necessity of becoming involved in a twelve-step program of recovery, they would still be providing chemically dependent people with the single most important guideline for potential recovery.

2. Al Anon, Alateen, and Related Organizations for the Codependent. Although until recently codependent people have received little professional attention, the grass-roots movement Al Anon--based on the twelve steps of AA--has been providing support to codependent persons for almost as long as the parent organization has been in existence. Additional services for families of chemically dependent people, including education and supportive therapy, can be obtained from many of the agencies that treat the chemically dependent.

3. Professional Referral Sources. The National Council on Alcoholism is perhaps the best-known referral agency. Other similar national and local organizations also make referrals and can relieve nonspecialists, including pastoral ministers, from making such decisions.

4. Alcohol and Drug Crisis Hot Lines. Another important resource, particularly for people in crisis, is the network of drug and alcohol telephone hot lines that one can call night or day. These organizations, often staffed by volunteers who are themselves in recovery, provide invaluable support, advice, and referral. Alcoholics Anonymous and other twelve-step organizations also provide volunteer phone coverage and personal assistance.

5. Residential Treatment Programs. These facilities offer programs that can last from a few days or weeks to several months, depending on the kinds of services provided. Shorter programs (usually less than seven days long) assist people to withdraw from alcohol or other drugs, a process termed "detoxification." Some "detox centers," as they are called, provide medical care, whereas others are supervised "drying our stations." Although some of these programs offer supportive counseling during the detoxification process, they are not designed to provide long-term support for recovery. After leaving the detox program, some clients join twelve-step programs; other obtain intensive rehabilitation at residential treatment centers.

The majority of residential programs, lasting a few weeks, offer comprehensive medical, educational, and therapeutic treatment. Most treat all forms of chemical dependency and apply a philosophy of therapy that relies heavily on AA and similar approaches. A few programs provide behavior modification to establish and maintain abstinence. Most of these regimens have been established in hospitals, and they are expensive. Residential treatment provides a preferable as well as effective option for many chemically dependent individuals, since they face the possibility of experiencing the life-threatening physical and psychological consequences associated with withdrawal.

Long-term residential programs of several months to a year or longer have been designed to treat the chemically dependent person within an environment isolated from negative social influences. To establish and maintain a high level of commitment to recovery, most of these programs espouse a unique, intense, confrontational treatment style. Many of these programs treat only narcotic addicts, but a few have opened their doors to people with other forms of chemical dependency.

Another type of long-term treatment facility, the "halfway house," has been designed to provide a chemical-free setting in which chemically dependent residents can give each other mutual support for recovery. In general, professional involvement in these houses has been slight. Recently, however, some of them have begun to offer individual and group therapy and to require attendance at twelve-step meetings.

Among the residential recovery programs, a few facilities have been established to meet the special needs of chemically dependent priests, women religious, and other religious personnel. Among these are the two Guest Houses in Michigan and Minnesota, St. Luke Institute in Suitland, Maryland, and Southdown in Aurora, Ontario, Canada.

6. Outpatient Counseling Programs. Recently, outpatient programs have been initiated by state, county, city, or private agencies to provide relatively low-cost treatment. These outpatient programs vary widely in the services they offer. Pastoral ministers might find it helpful to investigate the local programs so as to become familiar with those to which they can make appropriate referrals.

A LIFELONG TASK

The work of recovery continues throughout life for the chemically dependent man or woman, since theirs is a chronic disease that can only be arrested, never cured. In addition, they need to rebuild their personal lives, which have been damaged by years of chemical abuse. Continuing involvement with the fellowship of AA, or other twelve-step programs can provide the nucleus of the support that is required to achieve these difficult, long-term undertakings. Moreover, successful recovery depends on the continuing development of one's spiritual life, along with attention to physical and emotional needs. Pastoral ministers who make the efforts to acquire knowledge and sensitivity regarding the nature of chemical dependency and recovery can often serve as helpful sources of spiritual and emotional support for those who are recovering and rebuilding their lives.

This article originally appeared in Human Development 7.1 (1986): 39-42. Subscriptions to Human Development may be obtained by writing to P.O. Box 3000, Dept. HD, Denville, NJ 07834. A one year subscription, payable in US dollars, is $20.00 ($27.00 foreign). We are especially grateful to Human Development for setting aside their policy of not allowing reprints for commercial purposes so that this essay could be reprinted here.

THE MINISTER AND ALCOHOLISM

The Reverend Bernard Pennington

Pennington argues that with God's help ministers can assist alcoholics in their struggles. He cites examples of how ministers have felt defeated in their attempts to work with alcoholics before providing suggestions on how to more effectively work with them.

The following is from a fairy tale titled "The Frog Pond" by Joyce MacIver. "Once there was a little man--and he led a little life--and one day he began to pack a little bag. And they said, "Where are you off to? Where are you going?" and he said, "I'm packing my bag and I'm going to Connemara." And they said, "You mean, you're going to Connemara, God willing." And he said, "I mean I'm going to Connemara." So God changed him into a frog and put him in a frog pond and kept him there for seven years. And then God changed him back again--and what did the little man do? He began at once to pack his little bag. And they said, "Where are you off to? Where are you going?" and he said, "I'm going to Connemara." And they said, "You mean, you're going to Connemara, God willing." And he said, "I mean, I'm going to Connemara, or back to the frog pond!"

Such is the problem which faces the clergyman today who would address himself to the problem of alcoholism. It is a very stubborn disease rooted in the early formation of a man's nature. The disease expresses itself in the attitude "come hell or high water, I'll take another drink if it kills me." At one time it would have been appropriate for the clergyman to stand in the pulpit and announce the wickedness of the drunk and his nefarious potion, and thus rid himself of responsibility relating to his wounded Samaritan. Not so today because in 1956 the Committee on Alcoholism of the American Medical Association described alcoholism as an illness needing the treatment of a physician.

At the same time, I was taught by a theologian that alcoholism was a disease, self-destructive in purpose, and in need of healing. So it is that present-day medicine, psychiatry and theology are teaching us an undeniable fact concerning alcoholism--that it is above all else primarily an illness, a disease, an act of self-destruction in need of the attention of the healing arts. Preaching at, talking to, telling what he "ought" to do, moralizing, and authoritarian relationships will no longer serve as the way to help the alcoholic.

It is a stubborn, unconscious process aimed at self-destruction. Most of the time we think of self-destruction as a pull-of-the-trigger, take-the-pill act that ends it all in a moment, such as in an instance of suicide. However, if a person engages in a series of activities causing injury or harm to one's self that person has entered upon a course of self-destructive acts which may be a "snow-balling" process. According to a thesis proposed by Karl Menninger several years ago in his book Man Against Himself, a person may reach a point in life experiences when he is tempted to enter into a series of acts that indicate movement toward self-destruction even though he would not consciously consider suicide. This thesis is dramatically demonstrated through chronic alcoholism. Actions are maintained that serve as solvents for bad feelings: this is reinforced by social action and social condemnation. "Alcoholism is of such a nature that no amount of resolutions on the part of the individual, or love for others, or persuasion by force, will stop the compulsive desire for drink." For the alcoholic, it is, "I am going to Connemara or back to the frog pond."

Certainly, when this is the attitude of the drinker, and when the compulsion to drink is this strong, then the consumer of alcohol has become a victim of the disease of alcoholism. That is, a process which is unrelenting and implacable unless something is introduced of greater strength to stop it. Self-destruction is on the way, and the person may die of excessive consumption of alcohol.

This all leads us to the statement that alcoholism is a confrontation to the minister. The severity and complexity of the problem are ever confronting the parish minister. I had an opportunity to talk to several clergymen recently about their work with alcoholics, and about their concerns in regard to alcoholism. This is what the clergymen told me:

Pastor V. was talking with me the other day, saying, "In fifteen years I have had only one successful relationship with an alcoholic. This man got interested in the church and he is still hard at work there. The rest have all gone back to drink. It is, personally, the least rewarding group of people I have ever known to work with. When it comes to the alcoholic I just throw up my hands." Pastor V. then proceeded to tell me of a situation in which he had failed. It seems that Alcoholic Charles had come faithfully to church for two weeks and then "all of a sudden for no reason at all" had turned up with a bottle in the pastor's study: at this, Pastor V. took Charley to the state hospital's program for alcoholism.

Pastor W. made this statement: "There is one in my church who is tearing up his home. He is a very wealthy man, and can materially afford to drink, but meanwhile his son is going off his rocker. The boy comes to me and tells me of his great fear that he will be like his father. The tragedy here for me is that I cannot approach the man on the subject of drink. He has walled me off. He seems to feel that he has got everything in hand. I just don't know what to do. I can see the destructiveness but there is nothing I can do about it."

Pastor X. made this statement: "They come to me but I just don't know what to say or give them that will make any difference. I usually just make it a point to work with other people."

Pastor Y. was talking, and he stated that the thing that bothered him the most was in regard to the moral issue at hand: "When is the guy sick, and when is he just a drunk who is stubborn and needs a kick in the seat of the pants and be told to grow up?"

Pastor Z. expressed concern for the alcoholic, saying that he was aware of the church's influence and inability to cope with the problem. He said, "The thing that bothers me most is that the church is not available as a redemptive community and fellowship."

The problems here from the perspective of the ministry are obvious, and they are serious. Let me list them:

1. The minister is confronted with a baffling situation of human suffering and destruction that prevents his help.

2. The minister is confronted theologically in regard to his understanding of sin and sickness as pertaining to the alcoholic.

3. He is confronted with regard to the church being, in actuality, and I quote Pastor Z.: "The redemptive community and fellowship of love and acceptance." How is the saving grace of God available to the alcoholic?--is Pastor Z.'s question.

4. Pastor X. was confronted with a complete empty-handedness and a feeling of inadequacy in regard to the alcoholic, and some of us feel just like him.

5.   The alcoholic confronts us with a feeling of being unrewarded in light of the great output of energy required to work with him and the gains seemingly made.

These are all important issues for the minister, and they challenge the integrity of his pastoral ministry.

Before we proceed further to the examination of these confrontations made upon the minister, let us turn the coin over and look at how the minister confronts the alcoholic: Let us look at the minister as he might be seen by the alcoholic.

1.   He is probably seen as a person and symbol of self-control and power. A person above all other persons who is not a slave to drink and whose life is in good order.

2.   He is a person who belongs and who holds an accepted, admired, and esteemed position and place in society.

3.   He is one who deals with problems of guilt, of forgiveness and of love. (Problems that are very perplexing and troublesome to the alcoholic.) How often I have heard the alcoholic say: "I feel ashamed to sit down and talk with one when I think of all of the things that I have done."

4.   The minister may stand for something quite negative to the alcoholic, such as one who condemns. This may be why so many alcoholics feel the condemning and judgmental finger of the church. In other words, not so much because it is there, but because within they are so crowded with guilt and condemnation. It is only fair to say that many times the guilt and condemnation are reinforced by the ministry and the church.

Up to this point, we have shown and stated that alcoholism is a problem of self-destruction, a disease. We have presented this as a very confronting, baffling and perplexing problem to the minister and one which challenges him. We have also stated that the minister for the alcoholic is a confrontation, a positive one, and sometimes a negative one, positive in the sense that he can be a helper, and negative in the sense that often he stands for the condemning one. In short, then, the essence of our problem is that the minister must be enabled to actualize the **positive image** for which he stands and can **potentially** be experienced. **This** is often distorted due to the seemingly unbreakable wall of isolation thrown up by the disease. Such a wall of isolation is illustrated in the words of Dr. Alfred Acrin of Atlanta, Georgia, who said: "However, the very use of the word **alcoholic** has taken on such meaning recently as to make it literally a means of blocking off any possibility of treatment rather than encouraging it. For example, many people who profess themselves alcoholics, do so primarily to block others who are not alcoholics from helping them: in this way they maintain their feelings of **wishing** help and yet at the same time not being able to get it, by effectively stopping other people from helping them. When an alcoholic says to me, 'you don't drink, yourself, so you probably don't really understand,'--He is effectively thumbing his nose at me. While I would not object to his doing so, I would certainly doubt the possibilities of being able to help if he continues to do so." Very often the alcoholic's isolation is furthered by society. The person, alcoholic, has a low opinion of himself to begin with: His self-evaluation attitude is one of: "I am no good. I am a drunk. I have been kicked out of my home--I have lost my family--I cannot hold a job--and society says that's right scum, keep going." (Equals the reign/state of condemnation!) There is nothing to break the self-evaluative attitude resulting in the downward spiral and the completeness of the isolation. This sort of isolation will continue to be true until society can begin to act differently in relation to the alcoholic.

In light of these preventing factors, how is the minister to proceed to actualize the positive image in which he may be seen and minimize the negative? Whereas on the one hand there is one who is in need of help, his acts of self-destruction cry out greatly and vividly to all who see him: On the other hand, the minister, has help to give, and wants to meet on a receiving-giving plane to the one in need. As it is both embarrassing and confronting to him who is a representative of the free, reconciling and healing grace of God, **we need to broaden our concepts in understanding of the alcoholic and ourselves so that we are more equipped as pertaining to our knowledge and understanding** of our attitudes in relating to the alcoholic. This is our first step toward helping. Let me describe alcoholism to you from **several perspectives** as part of our thinking together about the nature and the depth of the disease.

1. I once heard a psychiatrist describe alcoholism as a problem of relatedness. The description went something like this: If alcoholism is to be understood as a problem, it must first be recognized as a solution to a problem. If drinking can be used as a means of solving a problem, can the problem be identified? What is it? Briefly stated thus: How to live reasonably comfortable in relation to one's self and to others. The problem drinker usually feels isolated or separated from himself, his environment, and the people who share it with him. This includes his family, his friends, his associates at work and play, and nearly always his church. 'No man is an island unto himself,' the poet writes, and yet to stand alone in a changing world and still feel a part of

everything is so seemingly contradictory that it is little wonder that so many fail in the struggle to resolve this problem, to achieve that feeling of relatedness. The implicit emotional growth and maturity is difficult indeed. He who resorts to alcohol to help solve this paradox becomes even more disillusioned when its use ultimately fails him. The person, then, who drinks uncontrollably, even into the state of oblivion, appears to be trying to isolate himself . . . he is not. He is trying no matter how unsuccessfully or antisocially to promote a feeling of relatedness; to achieve relatedness and mutual understanding whether with an individual or with a group brings to relationship a balm and nourishment like sunshine and rain to plants. Against this feeling of being someone and feeling related to others, alcohol is a poor competitor.

2. From a phenomenical perspective, we can understand another dimension of the disease. Dr. Masserman gives us these words: "Consider puny man: blessed with almost boundless imagery, but cursed since Paleolithic times with an intelligence that perceives about him a vast, chaotic, infinitely threatening universe, ready at any moment to harm or destroy him. What basic defense can, must, he evolve, else suffer from anxiety so deep and pervasive that life would be intolerable?" Such is the inward condition of the alcoholic. He is a man suffering from anxiety so deep and pervasive that life, as he knows it, is intolerable: that only through the screen and illusion created by alcohol is he able to live.

3. Theologically, we would say that the alcoholic is a sinner, and in need of salvation. This implies that he is lost, separated from God, the ground of his being--in need of new birth--new attitudes himself and life around him. The old issue of compliancy vs. surrender becomes very clear in theological context. Surrender is a form and a part of the

new birth process. It is accepting the experience of one's humanness, one's separatedness and one's need for being reborn. When a man is born again, he hits the bottom and starts all over again on a new way of life and growth. In theological terms, compliancy is a form of "Phariseeism"--it is an intellectual assent and a compulsive energy aimed towards not surrendering himself but maintaining one's self in the face of relentless disease. In phariseeism/compliancy, the head says "yes" but the heart/feelings are not yet ready to give in to the condition of being lost and in need of rebirth/surrendering. When we say the alcoholic is a **capital S sinner**, we imply that small s, sins are primarily symptoms and acts of omission/commission. A capital S sin is primarily a condition representing a state of separation/isolation. The so-called sins of life are symptoms of the condition of separation and isolation. Because of man's isolation he endeavors to compensate in every way possible, hoping to save himself (compliancy) from the lack of relatedness that he feels and from deep anxiety that he experiences and from the suffering that he knows. There is probably no other illness which so vividly illustrated the condition of capital S, sin and the resulting sickness as in the instance of alcoholism. "The person who is to become an alcoholic is born thrust into a world of confusion, separated from the mother in helplessness. Instead of experiencing the love that would help bridge the isolation gap, and reunite him with the grounds of his being, he begins to experience rejection, and thus is started on the path of self-destruction and self-hatred. The gap between himself and wholeness is widened; in short, he is lost in sin." Thomas McDill a theologian has written these words: "When sin is not understood as a state of separation, it is invariably treated by laws. Laws may restrain, and in this we must have laws, but this is not redemption; this is not salvation. You may keep someone from murdering, but you do not redeem the murderer by this restraint. You may keep someone from stealing, but you do not redeem the thief by this restraint. You may keep someone from drinking, but you do not redeem the life of the alcoholic by this restraint." Salvation takes on meaning as a reunion of that which is broken, in short, the relationship between man and God. Paul Tillich has written these words as a description of salvation: "Salvation is basically and essentially healing, the reestablishment of a whole that has broken, disrupted and disintegrated." From this you can easily see that he who sees alcoholism as a sin to be condemned rather than a wound to be healed, is proceeding in such a way as to fail both in regard to himself and his calling to help the alcoholic.

On the other hand, he who proceeds on the basis of understanding alcoholism as the condition of capital S, sin, or sin as being symptomatic of that state of separation, of being lost, can approach the alcoholic and the severity of his resulting illness in a creative and redemptive manner, and promote the healing process.

When, therefore, the minister accepts the challenge of relating to the alcoholic, he must proceed on a creative basis, familiarizing himself with the behavior sciences and personality theories, and examining the insights of modern psychology, medicine, and theology. Let me discuss with you several (5) helpful points which may facilitate your ministry to the alcoholic, and help you actualize your positive image for him.

1.   Often, I think that we approach the alcoholic with unrealistic expectations. Such was the situation in the case of Pastor V. and the alcoholic Charles. It was very unrealistic to expect that alcoholic Charles could become a faithful church member in such a short time, having only

spent a few hours in the pastor's study. Another way to state this problem is to say that we expect the alcoholic to respond **just as if** he were not emotionally disturbed, just as if he were not ill, just as if he were an ordinary person, and of course this is not so. But when we do this, we further build the wall of isolation, for almost inevitably the alcoholic will not respond like the person whose ego is strong and capable of reality's many and continuous hard demands. It is under these demands of reality--responsibility--being a father, being a husband, raising children--that the alcoholic folds up, because the ego, inner resources of the alcoholic is often weak and fragmented. He has an adult body, but nearly all else about him is infantile. It is quite often in light of this adult body that we are trapped into expecting him to be an adult, when all the while he simply is not capable of continuously performing as one. When the pain of the alcoholic's disease strikes him, he **will not** respond to responsibility, **nor will** he value himself nor any other person so much that he will not turn to drink. We expect the alcoholic to be responsible like other non-alcoholics and of course when we do, we set ourselves up for feelings of failure and inadequacy, and feelings of condemnation toward the alcoholic for not living up to our expectations. Our ministry to the alcoholic must be characterized by our letting him know where we stand in relation to what we have to offer him. In other words, let him know from the beginning what to expect and then stick to it. Understanding the alcoholic in terms of what he is capable of in light of his illness does not exclude having faith and confidence in him as a person.

    2. Set for the relationship with the alcoholic realistic goals **rather** than thinking of success in terms of his being totally healed, made whole, saved, and totally a responsible person. (Like, who is?) Think of success in terms of a

relationship of sustaining and guidance. Sustenance through life crises aims towards and produces personal growth and wholeness. Sustenance is a ministry of support and encouragement through standing by when what has been whole has been broken or impaired and is incapable of total situational restoration or at least not now. We can value a ministry sustaining and guidance by recognizing that sustaining and guiding are always pointed toward and geared toward healing and/or wholeness. The following is an example of sustenance: (Hilda Mushanki) "After the Germans had entered my country and the atrocities started, I felt for some weeks completely perplexed, wondering whether the whole world had become crazy, but after some weeks I could not help but realize that it was not I who was crazy, but that everything that was happening around me was a dreadful reality, and that it was not going to stop soon. Then a deep depression came over me, and I started wondering whether it was really worthwhile to live and to raise children in a world where all achievements of a many-thousand-year-old culture could be deserted as fast, as easily and as thoroughly as I was forced to witness. In this critical moment I was approached by members of the resistant movement, and the faith and the courage of the men gave me back my own courage and my willingness to live." We (you) are, the victims of alcoholism, men who can call forth, by ministry of sustenance, the courage and willingness to live.

3. There is the quality of a meaningful relationship for the alcoholic and the minister represented in standing by him, being available to him as a real vs. role person. The alcoholic is like a man swimming in the ocean with no ground in sight on which he can stand. Many times he can swim for days, weeks, and months, and sometimes even for years, and some end up swimming forever until they die

(miserable life though it be), but many, in fact the most, become tired of swimming and drown. The minister can be to the alcoholic, in his relationship to him, a solid ground on which he can regain his footing and gain strength to face the anxieties and the vicissitudes of life. The minister can be supportive. He can be a source of sustenance that calls forth the strength and courage which will help the alcoholic on to being a new being. All of which is dependent on the minister's being a source of **real communication as a real person** who **really cares** and who is also a minister. The reality of being a real person must not be contradictory to the role of being a minister. These two must be well integrated, not paradoxical, but wholesomely compatible in being real objects with the alcoholic. He knows us as human beings **who struggle, have feelings** and who **cope with life** in **constructive, hopeful ways.** He knows us as brothers who are in many ways, like him in the sharing of our real selves with him, through personal communication. We give him something of hope and strength.

4. To be a real person, real objects with the alcoholic is not contradictory to being ministers to the alcoholic. We carry within our role symbols of power, symbols of God's almighty love, knowledge, and powerfulness. We carry in our roles symbols of God's relationship to the world. We must try to personify these in our person and in our roles, thus using our roles as a form of ministry; drawing on its symbolic and real power for those who have lost sight of, and feel separated from the God that we represent.

5. Be available to the alcoholic on a primary rather than a secondary level of relating. Let ne now tell you what I mean by this terminology. On the primary level of relating the dynamics are geared to the instinctual needs, and on the secondary level the dynamics are geared to the social needs. Most forms of relating today in regard to the alcoholic are

secondary, that is, they are ego-oriented. However, many alcoholics have less ego available to them, and are more dominated by their primary needs, their instinctual needs. The alcoholic's behavior is dominated by normal, natural needs which have never been met. Unlike the neurotic, who tries to repress and distort his basic drives, the problem drinker tries to destroy his. He sees these needs as being bad. He sees his needs, and these are the primary needs, dependency, love, sex, aggression, as being bad because they have never been met. He hates himself for feeling hungry and cold. Therefore, he needs someone to relate to him on a primary basis. This is sometimes called replacement therapy. In this kind of relationship, his vital, basic needs are met by acceptance, by care, by sustenance, by concern. You might remember in relating to the alcoholic that you cannot reason with hunger, because hunger requires only one thing, and that is not reason, that is (relational) food. Therefore, relate to the alcoholic in such a way as to feed his instinctual needs. Certainly, if you develop a ministry of giving sustenance, that of sustaining and guiding, you will be contributing to the vital, basic, primary needs of the person. More than anything else in the world, he needs acceptance, genuine and deep. He needs care. He needs, in short, the love of God which is in Jesus Christ our Lord.

In summary, we have said that the minister is confronted with the problem of alcoholism, a disease. We have said that he has something of great significance and value to offer toward the alcoholic's problem. We have given some suggestions which will help the minister in facing this confrontation when he accepts the challenge in relating to the alcoholic. William K. Anderson of the Christian Century wrote these words:

"I have seen a tangle of ants mired in the dregs of a honeyjar to which they had come to sate themselves in sweetness. I have seen the protecting globe of an electric light darkened by the dried remains of a thousand insects that had found death as they sought light. I have seen gorgeous sedans full of exuberant young people, shouting in glee as they streaked to meet death at the corner. I have seen those who once thought it was always fair weather when good fellows got together, gathered in huddles of consolation in the rainy days of later life, on street corners and in flophouses, poor-houses and asylums. I have seen two generations of civilized human beings using the magical products of a God-given science for self-destruction."

God helping us we can assist the alcoholic in his struggle to live a constructive life.

This article originally appeared in NCCA Blue Book *26 (1974): 60-69. It is reprinted with permission.*

FAMILY DYNAMICS

Joanne Holladay, CAC

*Estimates vary as to the number of
people affected by the alcoholic. But
there is no doubt that the families of
alcoholics suffer as a result of the
alcoholism. In this essay, Holladay
gives general information about the
family dynamics of alcoholism.*

It is my pleasure to present this workshop on Adult
Child and Family Dynamics. I believe I am eminently
qualified as the child of 2 alcoholic parents, a child alcoholic,
adolescent alcoholic, parent alcoholic and now have a 22
year old son who is a chronic alcoholic and an 18 year old
classic co-dependent daughter. My ex-spouse has gone on
to marry a sick woman and everybody's in therapy of one
kind or another. It's been 17 years since my last drink or
drug.

To review --symptoms and definitions:

1. PROGRESSIVE - Disease which has a known
   and predictable course and will continue to
   worsen unless the addicted person is intervened
   with and given professional help.
2. CHRONIC - It cannot be cured.
3. POTENTIALLY FATAL - An alcoholic will die
   12 to 15 years sooner than a non-alcoholic
   person.
4. IDENTIFIABLE SYMPTOMS - Include
   blackouts, loss of control, denial, preoccupation
   with alcohol, withdrawal symptoms, mood swings,
   behavior changes and poor eating and sleeping
   habits.

5.   LIFE DETERIORATION - Injures the person economically, socially, physically, psychologically and spiritually. His relationships break down, work performance is impaired, depression occurs often and his behavior goes against his values.

6.   UNKNOWN CAUSE - Is probably a combination of a number of factors.

Now as an alcoholic progress, the family, as is true in any dysfunctional family, begins to take unconscious defense roles.

CHEMICAL DEPENDENT
1. Perfectionist
2. Rigid
3. Blaming
4. Withdrawal (Em. & Phys.)

PRIME ENABLER
1. Super - Worker
2. Physical Illnesses
3. Overly Responsible
4. Low Self-esteem

FIRST CHILD - OLDEST CHILD
Family "Hero"
1. "Good Kid"
2. Successful
3. Works for Approval
4. Non-feeling

SECOND CHILD
"Scapegoat"
1. Values Peer Group
2. Chemical User
3. Low Achiever
4. Defiant
5. Unplanned Pregnancy

THIRD CHILD
"Lost Child"
1. Shy
2. Treasures Pets/Things
3. Loner
4. Sickly

FOURTH CHILD
"Mascot"
1. Hyperactive
2. Attracts Attention
3. Teases, Humor, Comic
4. Slow Learner
5. Sexually Permissive

I can attest to the accuracy of the roles. Today my son vacillates between the "scapegoat" and the "lost child." My daughter is compulsively Family Hero and Prime Enabler with a flavor of "Mascot."

The reason my poor family is still locked into the disease if simply they never received help of any kind--as this alcoholic recovered, soon she was replaced by another--the son.

The Problem

Many of us find that we have several characteristics in common as a result of being brought up in an alcoholic household. We came to feel isolated, uneasy with other people--especially authority figures. To protect ourselves, we became people-pleasers, even though we lost our identities in the process. Personal criticism is perceived as a threat. We either become alcoholics ourselves or marry them--or both. Failing that, we find another compulsive personality, such as a workaholic, to fulfill our sick need for abandonment. We live life from the standpoint of victims. We have an overdeveloped sense of responsibility and prefer to be concerned with others rather than ourselves. We somehow get guilt feelings if we stand up for ourselves rather than giving to others. Thus, we become reactors rather than actors; letting others take the initiative.

We are dependent personalities who are terrified of abandonment--who will do almost anything to hold on to a relationship in order not to be abandoned emotionally. Yet we keep choosing insecure relationships because they match our childhood relationships with alcoholic parents. Thus, alcoholism can be seen as a family disease, and we can see ourselves as "co-alcoholics"--those who take on the characteristics of the disease without necessarily ever taking a drink. We learned to stuff our feelings in childhood and keep them buried as adults through that conditioning. In consequence, we confuse love and pity and tend to love those we can rescue and--even more self-defeating--we became addicted to excitement in all our affairs, preferring constant upsets to workable relationships.

This is a description, not an indictment.

Moving to Adult Children

These characteristics seem to predominate:
1. They guess at what normal is.
2. They have difficulty following a project through from beginning to end.
3. They lie when it would be just as easy to tell the truth.
4. They judge themselves without mercy.
5. They have difficulty having fun.
6. They take themselves too seriously.

7. They have difficulty with intimate relationships.
8. They overreact to changes over which they have no control.
9. They constantly seek approval and affirmation.
10. They usually feel different from other people.
11. They are super responsible or super irresponsible.
12. They are extremely loyal, even in the face of evidence that the loyalty is undeserved.
13. They tend to lock themselves into a course of action without giving serious consideration to alternative behaviors or possible consequences. This impulsivity leads to confusion, self-loathing, and loss of control of their environment. As a result, more energy is spent cleaning up the mess than would have been spent had the alternatives and consequences been examined in the first place.

Options for Recovery

Alternatives and systems for recovery would include meetings of:

Children of Alcoholic Parents (C.A.P.S.)

Adult Children of Alcoholics (A.C.O.A.)

If self-help groups are utilized, additional counseling therapy would be helpful. Dr. Robert Ackerman approximates 2 years minimum to properly address the depth of the problems.

Thank you for your attention.

This article originally appeared in <u>NCCA Blue Book</u> 38 (1986): 77-82. It is reprinted with permission.

THE CLERGY AND THE FAMILY DISEASE

Al-Anon was established as a Twelve Step Program for the family and friends of alcoholics. This article on pastoral ministry has been approved by the Al-Anon Conference.

Alcoholism does not appear, progress or maintain itself in isolation. It is a family disease, and those who live in the presence of an alcoholic become quite damaged themselves. Not only are they emotionally involved with a sick person, as indeed they would be with any member of the family who becomes ill, but with alcoholism their involvement is deeper because this disease damages physically, mentally and spiritually all those who are touched by it. Confronted with these terrible effects, the clergyman can be of great help to family members if he is sensitive to the true nature of the problem and able to deal with it straightforwardly.

Counseling Spouses of Alcoholics

Often the wife or husband of an alcoholic, even though desperate for help, will refuse to acknowledge alcoholism as the problem. The sense of shame, the constant tension of not knowing what will happen next, and the resulting withdrawal and isolation contribute to making the spouse of an alcoholic difficult to approach. If counseling is to be effective, a clergyman usually has to lay the groundwork by explaining that alcoholism is a disease. In working with the spouse, he usually has a dual task: to secure an open admission of the existence of alcoholism and to help the individual realize that both partners are deeply affected by the disease.

One of the greatest services an enlightened clergyman can perform, once the presence of alcoholism has been acknowledged, is to suggest that the non-alcoholic partner take advantage of the tremendous resources of help and healing available in Al-Anon. The clergyman should himself be well enough acquainted with the program to understand its great potential for transformation and to overcome the conventional resistance of the non-alcoholic to "going public" with the problem. Once the spouse of an alcoholic has found the acceptance and understanding of the Al-Anon fellowship, emotional and spiritual growth begins, and the clergyman can observe a marvelous metamorphosis that in itself is a joy and an inspiration. The Al-Anon program teaches a change in attitude and style of living, and members of the fellowship who thus develop new priorities for their lives are able to make a significant spiritual contribution to any religious community.

In counseling the family affected by alcoholism, one of the most difficult tasks for the clergyman is to refrain from giving well-meaning but too-specific advice. Telling a spouse what he or she should do--in effect, making decisions for the family--is a serious mistake. If a family is led, or pushed, into a choice that is not fully accepted or believed in, the whole situation may be made immeasurably worse. Indeed, if the clergyman attempts to intervene or thwart the normal process of events, he may well prevent the very crises out of which a vital decision might be made that could even lead to a permanent solution. The role of the pastoral counselor is not to make decisions but rather to interpret what is happening. However much the counselor may wish to change a given situation, the only valid way he can do this is by learning and interpreting what is taking place (at the same time providing emotional support), and then allowing the family members to make their own choices and act out their own roles in the drama of life. Naturally, this difficult principle applies even to the family's decision to accept the help of Al-Anon, which cannot be forced on anyone, however needy.

This is not, however, to minimize or belittle the actual contribution of the counselor. The family's frequent lack of understanding of the forces at work in the interactions of alcoholism demands considerable insight and interpretation on the part of the counselor--and this amounts to much more than just passive listening. Such counseling is, in effect, two persons working together to explore and resolve a problem.

Indeed, one-to-one counseling on a purely individual basis is the pastoral counselor's most productive approach in this circumstance, rather than any concerted attempt at marital counseling in its conventional form. For the purpose of counseling a non-alcoholic spouse is **not** to preserve the relationship but to assist that individual toward recovery. Maintaining this focus requires great concentration and restraint on the part of the counselor, since the prospect of separation is the eventuality that most troubles many clergymen--and often tempts them to intervene inappropriately. The fact is that alcoholism rarely runs its course without some period when the partners in any alcoholic relationship are separated: a few months, even years, or permanently. Separation is so common--and so often misunderstood--that it deserves special discussion in any remarks addressed to counselors.

If separation occurs, there should be no attempt to promote quick, easy reconciliation. Indeed, considerable harm has been done by clergymen who have intruded on this process and have forced the non-alcoholic partner to return too soon.

Separation, when properly motivated, can spur the beginning of recovery from alcoholism, which then may be followed by a genuine reconciliation and the establishment of the first real relationship a couple has ever had. The basic problem is not that a couple may be separated for the moment if the disease is not brought under control, but that the marriage may end tragically in death or divorce. The only way for this progressive disease to be arrested is for the drinking to stop. If remaining in the relationship means, if effect, enabling the drinking to continue, the non-alcoholic partner is completely justified in considering separation, not only for the obvious personal benefit but also as a means of forcing the alcoholic to face reality and, perhaps, find recovery.

It is possible for a spouse to leave an alcoholic in love, rather than waiting for that love to be destroyed. No partner should be condemned for refusing to join an alcoholic in a suicide pact, and continued drinking for an alcoholic is exactly that--a form of slow, unconscious suicide. Moreover, in some instances, continuing to live with a drinking alcoholic may be so destructive that the family may be irreparably damaged. Still loving the alcoholic, but motivated by love of self and love of children, a spouse may separate to protect the entire family.

Strangely enough, alcoholism is the only major illness in which separation does not occur, as a matter of course, through normal medical procedures. If a husband becomes mentally ill, hospital care is initiated when the illness becomes severe. When a husband is incapable of caring for a tubercular wife, hospitals are available. In both instances, separation is effected by prolonged treatment and hospitalization. Yet when the non-alcoholic spouse is unable to cope with the physical and mental effects of alcoholism, it is often found that private hospitalization is beyond the family's financial needs or that public facilities are utterly inadequate. Most spouses are left to fend for themselves, and when they do seek help, rarely is it available in the form needed. We must either accept separation for the well-being of the family, or provide adequate care for the alcoholic.

Finally, it should be acknowledged that, in the majority of cases, separation has actually been a fact of life for some time. During the worst stages of alcoholism, the effects of the disease have caused the alcoholic partner to fail in many areas of responsibility. Indeed, his or her ability to "love, honor and cherish" may long since have vanished. The separation resulting from alcoholism really occurs when the alcoholic is unable or unwilling to keep the marriage vows (or to participate responsibly and lovingly in the relationship).

Counseling Children of Alcoholics

By far the largest group afflicted by alcoholism are the children. A conservative estimate puts their number at 12 or 13 million, many of whom are in danger of becoming alcoholic themselves without counseling and appropriate help.

It is earnestly recommended that the clergyman or pastoral counselor refer any youngster between the ages of 12 and 18 to Alateen, the program for teenagers which is an outgrowth of Al-Anon.

The children of alcoholics are not like other teenagers. Usually they have spent years living under the same roof with an alcoholic parent and have suffered from the illness in their own way. The children have endured their parents' tantrums, dreaded their excesses and accepted their moods. Only those who have lived with this situation can know it.

Most teenagers who come to Alateen feel they are the only ones in the world who have had to endure the uncertainties of alcoholism. Most have a fairly well-developed martyr complex. Most have long since decided that their parents did not want them, do not want them, or couldn't care less about them. Most of those who come to Alateen learn for the first time as a complete revelation that alcoholism is a disease. In Alateen meetings they meet others who have endured similar feelings of rejection. They meet those who have learned to cope with embarrassing situations because one or both of their parents are drinking. In Alateen, the young share experiences, solve mutual problems and assist each other in being the fine young people they are meant to be--and can be.

The clergyman or pastoral counselor may have to overcome certain obstacles in referring a youngster to Alateen. One of the greatest hindrances is parents. Many do not want their children to attend Alateen even though both parents may be enjoying the benefits and blessings of AA and Al-Anon. It is a great mistake for parents to underestimate their youngsters' seriousness of purpose, their earnest desire to learn how to live successfully despite the difficulties of alcoholism. The clergyman can do much to reassure the parents of the benefits of Alateen to the whole family and can allay their fears and embarrassment that the children have also been seriously affected by the family disease of alcoholism.

Teenagers themselves may show a reluctance to attend Alateen. They too are unwilling to face the difficult feelings associated with the drinking. It is easy to cite conflicts with homework, preparation for tomorrow's classes or a sports program as the reason why attending an evening Alateen meeting is impossible. Transportation is another problem, as most Alateens do not drive, and walking the streets at night can be dangerous. A solution to such problems may be in holding an Alateen meeting at the same time as an Al-Anon or AA meeting. In this way, getting help can be seen as a family affair. Without it, the emotional disturbance caused by having an alcoholic parent can have long-lasting effects. A clergyman should urge teenagers with alcoholic parents to attend Alateen as a top priority.

Conclusion

Virtually all members of families affected by alcoholism suffer from serious physical, emotional and spiritual problems. Fortunately, those who seek help through Al-Anon and Alateen are able to face those problems with new strength and perspective. They learn not to speculate fearfully about the future or brood over the past, instead dealing with each day--often each minute--as the time that really counts in their lives. Living one day at a time frees them to cultivate a new relationship with the God of their understanding, which in turn reinforces their sense of wholeness and acceptance.

As this spiritual growth occurs, they develop a greater sense of community, no longer isolating themselves because they feel hopeless and afraid. They discover a sense of concern for others, and seek to find ways to express that concern: their ministry to others has begun. Clearly, such individuals are an important spiritual resource for any religious community, in an era when so many people are fearful about the future.

From Al-Anon Faces Alcoholism, copyright 1981, by Al-Anon Family Group Headquarters, Inc. Reprinted by permission of Al-Anon Family Group Headquarters, Inc.

NEGLECT OF TRANSPERSONAL
UNFAIR TO CLIENTS

Reverend Donald P. Richmond

*Using the case of a native American woman as
an example, Richmond shows how therapists
who neglect the spiritual can harm their clients.*

For many years now the professional community has largely accepted the medical model of addictions. While bringing addiction out of the moral arena and placing it in the medical arena produced tremendous headway, in an effort to support this model we also have blindly accepted a medical approach to counseling.

We make no place in our sessions to discuss the divine. As professionals who loudly proclaim an eclectic approach to counseling, we avoid one most useful discipline--biblical counseling.

In her landmark work, The Forgotten Children, R. Margaret Cork wrote that " ...there was some connection between abstinence and church attendance."

Speaking much more boldly, Dr. Howard Clinebell said "...there is no area of human suffering in which religion has given a more convincing demonstration of its therapeutic power than in the problem of alcoholism." These are just two witnesses who testify to the "therapeutic power" of the divine in conquering addictions.

Other well-known supporters of such an idea are Carl G. Jung, Dr. Harry Tiebout, David Wilkerson, possibly William James, and the early founders of AA. With so great a host of witnesses, the question that should concern many addictions workers today is, "Why do we deliberately avoid the spiritual dimension in our counseling activities?"

For some, it is an issue of ethics, unfounded though that may be. Yet, it is important that we do not impose our spiritual bias upon another person, especially upon a client within a professional relationship.

That, however, is a far cry from preparing the ground for another to receive the "seed" of spirituality. A "seed" which, I might add, could be the key to the maintenance of continued sobriety. This being the case, an avoidance of life's spiritual dimension may in itself be the real breach of ethics.

Consider, for example, how we encounter addicted persons who are having problems with loneliness. Although loneliness may be considered one of many indicators of an addiction brought on by denial and withdrawing socially, it may be equally true that loneliness may be a predisposing factor of addiction. Addiction in the latter case only masks and aggravates the original problem of loneliness.

This loneliness may be caused by a wide variety of factors such as early childhood experiences, present isolation, undeveloped or unused social skills, or a **sense of separation from the spiritual dimension of life.** How do the medical, humanistic, or behavioral models of counseling prompt the client into achieving a healthy transpersonal experience? Quite frankly, they cannot. "Referral" to someone who can prompt such an experience is all too often a pathetic refrain. Even our eclecticism does not prove to be a sufficient base.

Consider, also, the case of a young Native American person who comes into the office. She presents her problem as addiction, and during the course of the initial interview we discover that she has been "hearing and seeing things." We may believe these hallucinations are the result of chemical abuse. Or, she may be experiencing psychotic episodes.

But upon further examination we could discover that she has always had these experiences and that her family is very involved in native religious practices. What would you do?

To be safe I would refer her (upon her request) to a psychiatrist, but I would want to make certain that professional did not consciously or unconsciously seek to demythologize life.

We need to be careful that such a young person not be wrongly classified as a psychotic when, in fact, she may have had valid transpersonal experiences. Most professionals do not believe in these experiences--to them there is no spiritual dimension. This is a most unfortunate position to hold considering the mounting evidence on behalf of a spiritual reality.

To maintain our effectiveness as addictions counselors, we must: reconsider our materialist opinions and be receptive to an "open" universe; rework our counseling philosophy and practice to include a spiritual dimension--man is body, mind, and spirit, and we must not avoid the third dimension; be well read on issues relating to the transpersonal, including Biblical counseling.

This article originally appeared in Alcoholism and Addiction Magazine 8.4 (1988): 22. It is reprinted with permission.

For Further Reading on
Ministry to Alcoholics and Their Families

Anderson, G. W. (1982). Candid Concern: The Church's Ministry to the Chemically Dependent Person (Alcoholism). Engage/Social Action, 10, 15-19.

Anderson explains why ministers, priests, and rabbis have been ineffective in working with alcoholics. He suggests ways in which clergy can better minister to alcoholics.

Bergendoff, C. (1981). Pastoral Care for Alcoholism: An Introduction. Center City, MN: Hazelden.

Bergendoff gives general information about alcoholism before explaining the pastor's role and opportunity in working with alcoholics and their families.

Bissell, L., & Royce, J. E. (1987). Ethics for Addiction Professionals. Center City, Minnesota: Hazelden.

Bissell and Royce include information on patient rights, economic issues, professional relations, and AA traditions.

Block, M. A. (1962). The Clergy. In M. Block, Alcoholism. (pp. 254-257). New York: John Day Company.

Block believes that "Perhaps no group can serve the alcoholic patient more effectively than the clergy." He gives specific advice to ministers who work with alcoholics. He also points out the importance religion plays in recovery.

Buck D. (1971). Cooperate with AA. NCCA Blue Book, 23, 25-32.

Buck accepts the idea that "the first person to get an inquiry about alcoholism is a member of the clergy." He argues that the best referral that the member of the clergy can give the alcoholic is to AA or to a member of AA.

Clausen, W. (1987). Homily--June 22, 1987. NCCA Blue Book, 39, 105-110.

Clausen reports on how he organized a Sobriety Sunday for his parish.

Del Genio, T. (1984). Parish Ministries to Alcoholics. NCCA Blue Book, 36, #10.

Sr. Del Genio explains about the alcohol education programs which were set up in her parish. Lay ministers were the core of these programs. The need to educate seminarians also received special attention.

Dolan, L. (1984). Campus Ministry. NCCA Blue Book, 36, #16.

Dolan discusses his work as campus minister before describing his own addiction and recovery.

Doman, L. (1970). The Church and Prevention of Alcoholism. Journal of Religion and Health, 9(2), 138-161.

Doman argues that (1) "The church should strive toward the improvement of community resources for the alcoholic." (2) "The church should mobilize a group of trained lay counselors [and ministers] for alcoholic prevention," and (3) "There are religious dimensions involved in alcoholic rehabilitation."

Dooher, G. B. (1986). Pastoral Care of the Chemically Dependent. Human Development, 7(1), 39-42.

Dooher explains that alcoholism is a serious problem that comes up in pastoral ministry. He explains how to identify the problem, how to confront the dependent person, and the types of treatment which abound.

Ford, J. (April 1955). Clerical Attitudes on Alcohol: Most of them Wrong. The Priest,

Fr. Ford identifies and explains five typical attitudes which ministers have toward alcohol: Unformed, uninformed, misinformed, deformed, and reformed.

Harrison, J. (1977). Church and Alcoholism: A Growing Involvement. Alcohol Health and Research World, 1(4), 2-10.

Harrison explains what various denominations are doing to assist alcoholics. Clergy alcoholics and training for clergy working with alcoholics is emphasized.

Johnson, V. E. (1973). Clergyman's Handbook: An Introduction to Steps IV, V, and VI. In V. E. Johnson, I'll Quit Tomorrow. (pp. 161-168). New York: Harper and Row.

Johnson explains Step 4, Step 5, and Step 6 and then gives advice to members of the clergy working with AA-alcoholics.

Keller, J. E. (1966). Ministering to Alcoholics. Minneapolis: Augsburg Publishing House.

Keller has written this book because "The parish pastor is frequently approached for help with the problem of alcoholism. [but] Because of certain popular misconceptions, he may hesitate to become involved."

Kellerman, J. L. (1974). Pastoral Care in Alcoholism. In F. Seixas, & R. Cadoret (eds.), The Person With Alcoholism. (pp. 144-146). New York: Academy of Sciences.

Kellerman begins by saying why the alcoholic frequently avoids the minister. He then describes how the minister can be an effective pastoral counselor by rooting his actions not in technique "but in his knowledge of God's love for himself and others."

Kenny, K. (1988). It Only Hurts When I Grow Up: Stories from Covenant House for Hurting Kids. New York, New York: Paulist Press.

Fr. Kenny provides a number of case studies of youth who were helped at Covenant House. Of particular interest are the cases of Johnny, whose father was an alcoholic; Morey, a Jewish drug addict; and Jackson, a crack addict.

Kushner, P. (1980). The Role of the Rabbi. A. Blaine (ed.), Alcoholism and the Jewish Community. (pp. 305-309). New York: Federation of Jewish Philanthropies of New York.

Kushner offers suggestions to rabbis who work with an alcoholic congregant. But he stresses that before rabbis can offer assistance, they must first recognize that alcoholics do exist in their congregations.

Mann, M. (1951). The Pastor's Resources in Dealing with Alcoholics. Pastoral Psychology, 2(13), 11-19.

Mann writes that "the purpose of this article [is] to explain the working of Alcoholics Anonymous as a method of recovery." In doing so, she not only explains the spiritual role of the program, but also the relationship of a non-alcoholic pastor to the local AA group. Questions which pastors might have about AA are anticipated and answered.

Martin, J. C. (1973). No Laughing Matter: Chalk Talks on Alcohol. 1946; Cambridge: Harper and Row.

Fr. Martin explains basic treatment issues involved in working with alcoholics.

McDowell, F. K. (1972). The Pastor's Natural Ally Against Alcoholism. The Journal of Pastoral Care, 26(1), 26-32.

McDowell describes a family counseling program developed by the Kansas City National Council on Alcoholism.

Mehl, D. (Winter 1977). Facing Loss of Control. Military Chaplains' Review, 51-63.

Mehl, a recovered alcoholic minister, explains the process by which alcoholics lose control. He uses his own experience as a model. He gives special attention to the futility of controlled drinking. Specific suggestions are offered for working with alcoholics on these steps.

Morgan, O. J., & LaFair, S. (Spring 1985). The Family in Healing. Human Development, 20-24.

Fr. Morgan and Dr. LaFair argue that contextual therapy should be used when providing pastoral counseling to the child of an alcoholic. The case study of a woman whose father was an alcoholic is included.

(1982). Naval Chaplains Play a Role in Treatment. Alcoholism Update, 5(4), 7-8.

The article explains how naval chaplains are helping alcoholics.

Reidenbach, C. F. (1958). Pastor and the Alcoholic. Pastoral Psychology, 9(83), 9-12.

Reidenbach gives a general analysis of the role of the minister in helping alcoholics. He argues that religion should be a promise and not a threat.

Schmidt, C. (1970). The Bar Ministry. In D. J. Randolph (ed.), The Swinging Church. (pp. 80-98). Nashville: Tidings.

Schmitt, a Methodist minister, explains how he ministers to people in bars.

185

Shoemaker, H. (1967). I Stand By the Door: The Life of Sam Shoemaker. New York: Harper and Row.

This biography includes a chapter called "A Rescue Mission and Alcoholic's Anonymous." Shoemaker was an early supporter of AA.

Spickard, A., & Thompson, B. R. (1985). Dying for a Drink: What You Should Know About Alcoholism. Waco, TX: Word.

The authors provide a comprehensive view of alcoholism and recovery from a Christian point of view. Addiction, intervention, recovery, and family issues are addressed.

Swift, C., & Beverly, S. (1985). Utilization of Ministers as Alcohol Counselors and Educators: Increasing Prevention and Treatment Resources in the Black Community. In R. Wright, &T. Watts (eds.), Prevention of Black Alcoholism. (pp. 182-198). Springfield: Charles C. Thomas.

Although it was not published until 1985, the article reports on a study which was conducted in the 1970s where black ministers were employed by the court system as alcoholism counselors.

Warner, M. D., & Bernard, J. M. (1982). Pastoral Counseling with Alcoholics and Their Families. Pastoral Psychology, 31(1), 26-39.

Warner and Bernard argue for a family systems approach when clergy counsel alcoholics and their families. "Specific family systems concepts are discussed and how they relate to the dysfunctional unit which houses an alcoholic" are explained.

White, P. (1988). Spiritual Direction for Adult Children of Alcoholics. NCCA Blue Book, 40, 38-56.

White presents five movements developed by Father Tom Hickey and explains them in terms of ACAs. Each movement is discussed in terms of self, relationships, significant other, image of God, prayer, and scripture. He hopes that with this information priests will be better able to minister to ACAs.

DIVERSITY AMONG ALCOHOLICS

CULTURE AND LANGUAGE IN THE TREATMENT OF ALCOHOLISM: THE HISPANIC PERSPECTIVE

Antonio Melus, Ph.D.

Family and community are important factors in the lives of Hispanics as well as other alcoholics. But the impact of family and community on Spanish speaking alcoholics is different than in the dominate culture.

Each summer, entire Washington, D.C. neighborhoods erupt with a feeling of "fiesta" as the approximately 150,000 members of that city's Spanish community join together for the annual Latino festival. During the celebrations, an observer can easily detect and respond to the strong sense of community and the richness of diversity demonstrated by "la comunidad Hispana."

Drawn from almost every Spanish-speaking group and nationality, the D.C. Hispanic community is not predominated by members of one particular culture. Nor is the community itself located in one specific area, but is clustered in the neighborhoods from Northwest Washington to suburban Maryland and Virginia.

One of the challenges presented to those who provide services to Hispanics in Washington is the need to make programs culturally relevant to the various Spanish-speaking populations covering a wide geographic area.

These considerations were important in the planning and inception of alcoholism prevention and treatment services provided by Andromeda, Inc., a local community health center. As a starting point, staff members reviewed both research studies on Hispanics and evaluative reports on programs serving Spanish-speaking clients. Although hard data was scarce (Pattison 1977), note was taken of Pearson's (1964) speculations that certain factors could improve the success rate in treatment: acceptance and cooperation of the entire family in the treatment process; respect and cooperation of doctors, nurses, and social workers; treatment by Spanish-speaking staff; and acceptance of alcoholism as an illness.

The primary focus arrived at was the optimal use of language and culture as basic tools of therapy. The program was designed to be both bilingual and bicultural to maximize its relevance for all potential clients, ranging from recent immigrants to long-term residents. The special cases of families with American Hispanic backgrounds were considered, since their problems are often related to cultural differences.

To make the program even more sensitive to Hispanics, the importance to the individual of the family and the community was stressed and the alcoholism program was oriented toward these two social systems.

"La Familia"

The importance of the role that the Hispanic family (extended or nuclear) plays in the life of the individual cannot be underestimated. Duran (1975) sees "la familia as a source of emotional strength and well being." The current trend of the helping professions to treat the whole family as a unit, rather than as separate individuals, is quite relevant when applied to Hispanics because of the interdependence of the extended and nuclear family.

In treating the family, it is necessary to realize that there are specific familial patterns in the different Hispanic groups. For example, the relationship between mother and son is exceptionally close and dependent among Mexicans and Cubans. And Peruvians and Bolivians experience a stronger commitment to parents and siblings than to their spouses and children.

Alcohol abuse has a tremendous impact on these families, not only because of the negative social consequences such as violence, abuse and neglect of children, unemployment, high rates of death and disease related to alcoholism, and poverty, but also because of the tendency of alcoholism to cross several generations in the same family. Alcohol is also a factor in many cases of separation and divorce, thus further damaging the family structure.

Thus, whatever therapeutic approaches are used should be consistent with cultural values and mores if they are to be effective. In this case, the belief that the unity of the family is in danger because of alcohol abuse can have a compelling effect on all family members to change their behavior so that family unity will be maintained. Concepts like assertiveness, detachment, and independence, commonly effective tools when working with many alcoholics and their families, will rarely, if ever, be understood, much less accepted, by Hispanic clients, because those concepts are seen as a direct threat to the family.

If the alcoholic family member is a woman, the case usually is handled differently. The female Hispanic alcoholic finds much more rejection and greater stigmatization. She is often the victim of physical and/or verbal abuse from her family, so in these cases, the treatment approach must be more sensitive and cautious. If the alcoholic is a man, it is often easier to involve the family. But if it is a woman--and one-third of the program's clients are women--she is often reluctant to bring in her family, especially if the alcohol problem has not yet been openly identified.

"La Comunidad"

The need for a strong spirit of community is another characteristic of Hispanics, fulfilling a sense of identity and belonging. Hispanics tend to live together, work together, and spend free time together. The incidence of alcoholism within the Spanish community is high and the resource of that community must be marshalled behind prevention and treatment efforts.

To achieve this, strong community outreach efforts and close community involvement are utilized by Andromeda staff. These include sponsoring community picnics and parties with an emphasis on whole family participation. "Tardes Infantil" (afternoons for children) are held to teach young people about alcohol use and abuse. They are also encouraged to express their feelings about possible problems in their own families through painting, movies, and dramatizations. A local theater group and mime company participate in these activities.

Another way of making services relevant to this population was to establish a network of referrals to deal with problems often associated with alcohol abuse. In this way services were made more readily available to alcoholic clients who in turn identify and refer other new clients. The program works closely with AA and Al-Anon and serves as a referral agency for employment organizations.

As in many other programs working with minorities and substance abuse, Andromeda found one important function was its role of advocate and agent of change to help clients deal with the system. The system can be the source of the problem and also the source of the solution. It is important to educate people in how to use available resources and also to help agencies meet the needs of their clients, in this case, Hispanics.

"Lack of knowledge about alcoholism and a negative view of treatment are the basis for the negative attitudes and stigmatization that make alcoholism difficult to treat," says one Andromeda counselor. Attitudes and perceptions must be changed in the community to make treatment and prevention of alcoholism more successful.

References

Duran, R. La familia. The Chicano Plan for Mental Health, 1975, pp. 1-4.

Gutierrez, M.E. The Latino Family Linking the Past and the Present. Agenda, Jan. - Feb. 1979, pp. 8-10.

Pattison, E.M. Ten Years of Change in Alcoholism Treatment and Delivery Systems. American Journal of Psychiatry 134 (3): 261-265, 1977.

Pearson, A.W. El Tratamiento del Alcoholismo de Mexicanos que Viven en los Estados Unidos. (Treatment of alcoholism in Mexicans in the United States). Revista Mexicana de Psicologia 1 (4): 358-362, 1964.

This article originally appeared in Alcohol Health and Research World, Summer, 1980, pp. 19-20.

THE PLASTIC CHALICE:
ONE WOMAN'S ADVICE TO CLERGY

Frances Nystrom

*Under a pseudonym, this alcoholic woman
gives information about how a pastor might
respond to the plight of alcoholic women.*

Try to imagine that you are hearing confessions. You
recognize the penitent by some inflection that is familiar,
even in her whisper. She has never come to you before for
her confessions, but you know that she is Mrs. X, whom you
have seen at many of the church functions. She seems
terribly agitated now, and her voice is shaking. In a moment
you hear why. He last confession was two weeks ago, and
since that time she has been drunk eleven times!

Shocked speechless, you remember a cartoon of Brother
Juniper's confession box, and on one wall the framed motto:
"Try not to sound surprised." You try not to. But eleven
times!!! And she had seemed to be such a nice lady! Far
more monstrous than a drunken priest, you feel is a drunken
woman. And the very worst of these is the drunken mother
of innocent children. A drunken mother is to you, as she is
to everybody, an abomination before the Lord.

Will you, screeching, tell her so? Some priests have.
That's only natural, too.

Natural, yes, Christ-like, no. So don't do it, ever. As
she already feels that way about herself--(why else would she
be kneeling there, so trembling, so remorseful?) --your verbal
lashing may be just the final straw which drives her to
suicide.

Give her, instead, good counsel. But can you? Unless
you understand alcoholism, you almost surely will:

1. Admonish her not to be self-centered, to consider the
effect her drinking must have on her family, to try to be a

good mother. (Your voice will draw hearts and flowers around the "mother.") Or:

2. Suggest moderation--one drink before dinner, and one more, perhaps in the evening with her husband. Never more than three drinks during any given day! Or:

3. Remind her of the power of prayer, and ask that she stop in at the Rectory--SOON!--and take the Pledge for six-months or a year. Or:

4. Tell her to use her will-power; that it's a moral weakness to give in to a habit so degrading to a woman.

If any one of these sounds like a feasible suggestion to you, forget it! She has heard all this "advice" before, in confessions. It has been given often, and freely, and was worth exactly what she paid for it. Are you wondering if I follow poor Mrs. X around, to eavesdrop on her in the confessional? No need to eavesdrop, my friend. I've been poor Mrs. X in the confessional.

Poor Mrs. ____, Den Mother for a pack of Cub Scouts, Assistant Leader for the troop of Girl Scouts, twice-a-month cleaning-lady of the Holy Altar, an enthusiastic supporter of the Parent-Teachers' Organization, a member in good standing of the Christian Family Movement. And a "helpless, hopeless" drunk!

I so happily put quotation marks around the "helpless and hopeless" because I don't have to take a drink anymore.

Today's priests are doing as much for their parishioners. Growing numbers of seminarians and priests are becoming knowledgeable about the disease of alcoholism, and treat the alcoholic with understanding and compassion.

Not so in these early days! In dozens of articles I used to read: "Discuss your personal problems with your physician or clergyman." I did. I discussed mine with doctors, many of them, and stuffed myself with their tranquilizers. And kept on drinking. I discussed it in many confessionals and was so often sneered at (oh, yes, you can hear a sneer) and snarled at and screeched at, that eventually I began to feel nauseated at the sight of a Roman collar. Only two priests even mentioned AA to me, and that quite vaguely. Priests just simply washed their ecclesiastical hands of me, sooner or later.

In spite of all I said, they insisted on believing that my drunkenness was voluntary. It wasn't. I could no more stop at three drinks than you could stop falling after three feet if you jumped off the roof of a seminary. Difference is, you don't have to jump, but I did have to drink. That's what never seemed to get through to anyone: I did not want to take a drink; I had to.

I didn't know it then, myself, but I was in the clutches of advancing alcoholism. Ordinary drunkenness is to alcoholism what a breeze is to a typhoon. Garden-variety drinking, even if it is willful drunkenness, is like drifting gently down the stream in a row-boat. On this lazy river you can row, row, row you boat back to the shore again, any time you want to. Merrily, merrily, merrily, merrily; life is but a dream. Compulsive alcoholic drinking is like being swept over Niagara Falls. All your rowing, though you put into it all your strength and you will, can't keep you from going anywhere but down. Life is no more drifting and dreaming. It's a plunging into a nightmare now. Down into hell! And alcoholism is the coldest, sickest, loneliest hell in the world. Unless you find real help in time the only way out of it is escape by death, or through the vegetable-like insanity of a "wet brain."

What is so ironic is the fact that the help has been available since 1935! Why is it taking so long for the medical profession and the clergy to find out about it? If a man is going to be in a position to guide people through the desert of life, he should find out where the oasis is. In the case of the alcoholic, the oasis is listed in the telephone directory under Alcoholics Anonymous.

If every priest knew at least this much - that (1) alcoholism is compulsive, (2) it is almost impossible to achieve sobriety on one's own, and (3) that Alcoholics Anonymous will send someone to talk to the still-suffering victim if he will only dial the listed number for help - think how effective the priest could be as an instrument of the Holy Spirit.

An expanded version of this article originally appeared in <u>*NCCA Blue Book*</u> *22 (1970): 145-158. It is reprinted with permission.*

ON MY TWO YEAR BIRTHDAY

Suzanne Hendrich

*We live in a society which assumes that certain
people, such as lesbians or gay men, reject
healthy spiritual expression. Yet the lesbian
author expresses gratitude for her higher power.*

Did you see the woman who wanted to be a cake?
The cake in the window, so perfect and still.
Every bakery has one.
Icing rose petals like eggshells pale and cracked.
Visible dust on the white background,
The fragile art overwhelmed.
Relentless.
Life.
Its changes mark those who cannot change.

When I was a girl they made me change.
Out of tee shirts, out of blue jeans.
Into appropriate dress for a lady.
Into refinement, the pedestal perfect.
Out of exuberance, appetite, heroism.
Into stunned silence, reticence, fear.
I tried to change back but they just wouldn't let me.
I found something new, the love of a woman.
Equal and free we would feast and fly.
But they just wouldn't let us. They extracted a price.
The lesbian price is a bottle of gin
and how drinking it in can wash you away.
I was numb with the chill of crushed ice on glass,
no nourishing bowl to restore warmth.
I was numb to the bone with confusion.
I could not respond to an insult or to love (my broken
dream).

I could not dream   but I could experiment.
If this doesn't work then try something else.
Try beer if gin fools you. Try not drinking at home.
Try giving it up and see how that likes you.

It didn't like me

But I was in love
with a woman who felt things,
who felt things that I'd never known.
And I wanted that more than anything.

I was in agony, but it was a feeling I couldn't deny.
I suffered for what I didn't have, either drinking or her.
It was the same pain.

I loved that woman beyond my bounds, for along with her
came my
    feelings again:
surrender to appetite, natural world.
Today I can feel, I can cry, I can breathe
the light air of freedom until I'm full.
I can crash around in the underbrush of my past, unscathed,
looking
    for treasure.
Today I can take precious moments to let someone help me
know
    who I am
and I can be forgiven.
I can move on.
I can own my acts.
I can change
every day
I can know the best in me

and let it shine.

Let it shine.
The heroic light of foolish women
who give up everything to be free.
Let it shine.
A feast of lights.

Today I will eat the cake.
Life.
Relentless.
Whose changes mark those who could not change
but did.

This poem orignally appeared in <u>Out From Under: Sober Dykes and Our Friends</u> which was edited by Jean Swallow. It is reprinted with permission from Spinsters/Aunt Lute Book Company, Box 410687, San Francisco, CA 94141. The book sells for $8.95.

BLACK SPIRITUALITY AND RECOVERY FROM ALCOHOLISM

Carl M. Carlson III
Steven L. Berg

Unfortunately, the problem of discrimination in treatment programs cannot be denied. Fortunately, church based education/treatment strategies can work. This essay explains the problem which black alcoholics encounter and offers suggestions as to how to work with them.

The health needs of the black alcoholic is a major national issue and should be looked at more closely. A study done by the Secretary of Health and Human Services "identified chemical dependency as one of the six causes of death that contribute to a significantly lower life expectancy among minorities in comparison with the white majority." (Ronan, 1986-87, p.38) Unfortunately, when individuals think of chemical dependency, "concern is focused on the severe destruction caused by crack/cocaine and other illicit substances, [while] alcohol continues to destroy individual lives and families in the African-American community at a greater proportion than all illicit drugs combined." (Dozier, 1989, p. 33) In part, as a result of the emphasis being placed on illegal drugs, alcoholism in the black community, regrettably, has yet to be a popular national issue.

During the early history of the United States, slave-owners used alcohol as a controlling instrument. Alcohol was given in great volume to slaves on holidays as a reward for obedience and hard work; slave-owners hoped in this way to prevent any attempt toward rebellion. (Douglass, 1892) The abuse of alcohol was considered to be normal on those occasions. Some masters would reward slaves with alcohol or permit them to buy alcohol for themselves, but the extent of this practice is unknown. (Lender and Martin, 1982) Even after emancipation, alcohol was used as a way in which the majority population could control blacks (Lee, 1944; Franklin, 1974; Staples, 1976). Although not explicitly stated, the findings of recent studies of marketing alcohol in black communities suggests that efforts are still being made to exploit and control the black community with alcohol (Hacker and others, 1987). Williams (1982a) and Davis (1974) have suggested that alcohol abuse may have become a way of coping with major changes in the environment.

Alcoholism is a disease that affects not only the alcoholic, but all of the people to whom that person has close relationships (Holladay, 1986). A popular cliche is that alcoholics don't have relationships, they take hostages. The reality of this cliche can be seen in the divided loyalties which daughters of alcoholics have (Brisbane, 1986-87) and in Renita Weems (1987) moving story of the relationship with her alcoholic mother. Alcoholism, without discrimination, invades the lives of those who are in contact with it, causing pain, anger, and an overwhelming feeling of hopelessness. Yet, discrimination is too often found in treatment settings where black alcoholics and their families go for help.

Alcoholism always reveals itself to the alcoholic and loved one's in basically the same way, but it is not always caused by the same circumstances. Black alcoholism is not the same as another race's alcoholism in that physiological, psychological, sociocultural, ecological, and environmental backgrounds are inherently different. (Watts and Wright, 1983) For these reasons, not even all blacks can be put in the same category, but the problem of alcoholism in the Black-American community has a sociocultural history that makes it much more difficult to treat. (Bell, 1981) Or, as Brown and Tooley (1989) explain:

> While racial discrimination may be an overriding casual variable in the equation of mental health for blacks, its impact remains different for each subgroup. For example, for the middle income black, the drinking related issue may be alienation on the job; for the lower income black, it may be unemployment; and both may be mediated by racism.

Black alcoholism is an underrated, underresearched problem (Williams, 1982). In America, Blacks have historically suffered considerable discrimination, adverse circumstances, and oppression (Harding, 1981; Greene, 1969; Loewenberg and Bogin, 1976). Blacks cannot be expected to receive optimum care for alcoholism in a treatment center directed at white, middle-class, straight clients--the model for most U.S. treatment centers. In a study of nurses, Joan Artz (1976) found that "drug addicts, alcoholics, criminals, attempted suicides, very old people, homosexuals, welfare patients, and those viewed as minority group members" were distasteful patients. Clients who fall into more than one category, we can assume, become more distasteful. As such, it is not surprising that Thommie B. (1986), a black, gay alcoholic, experienced homophobia and racism not only in American culture, but in the gay community, the black community, and in the treatment community. Research done by Icard and Traunstein (1987) demonstrated that Thommie's personal experiences were not unique.

Lately, in the field of alcoholism, professionals are

finding that treatment must involve an understanding of the client's frame of reference in order to incorporate it into therapeutic methods to reach best results (Shilling and other, 1986; Cayleff, 1986; Miranda and Kitano, 1986). But to do this, we need to demand the development of stronger research programs to help alcoholism professionals and the black community better understand the needs of the black alcoholic. Dr. R.A. Winbush has argued that we should encourage all universities, especially historically black colleges to develop such programs (quoted in Williams, 1982).

Strong support systems such as AA are a proven and effective way to combat alcoholism in a variety of racial, ethnic, religious, and economic communities. Although some have suggested that AA does not work for blacks (Jones, 1980) AA is already working (Caldwell, 1983; Hudson, 1985-86) and there is a long history of black participation in AA (Hudson, 1978). Special interest meetings for black alcoholics in AA also exist and while racism does exist in some groups (Thommie, 1986) black participation has continued to break down racial prejudice among AA members.

The prevention of alcoholism in the black and other minority communities, should start at the grade school level and continue through the 12th grade. Such programs should train teachers to address alcohol information, values clarification, self-esteem, coping skills, and peer pressure to promote a positive self-image. Other prevention programs should include the training of peer leaders to conduct supervised activities among peers and other young people (Williams, 1982a and 1982b). In developing alcohol awareness programs, Harold A. Mulford (1970) cautions that individuals must first answer the question of "What Message presented by what means to what target population will change <u>what attitudes</u> and result in <u>what behavior?</u>" (p. 6)

In designing educational programs, the black church holds a unique position in the black community as both a seat of worship and healing (Levin, 1984). Historically, the church has been a center of the black community and religion has been a strong force in forming bonds within the community. Raboteau (1978) has described religion as the invisible institution in the antebellum south. In his book on <u>Slave Religion</u> he demonstrates how blacks used religious ideas to give meaning and structure to their world. In <u>Slaves Without Masters</u>, Berlin (1974) shows how free blacks clustered around their churches, churches that served not only as places of spiritual refuge, but also as a place where secular and social needs could be met. Looking at the contemporary black community, Knox (1985) has claimed that the church is "the most profound instrument available to blacks when it comes to coping with the multiplicity of problems that beset their lives." (p. 35) Given the spiritual nature of twelve step recovery programs, church involvement in alcohol education and prevention is especially valuable.

In the 1970s, Swift and Beverly (1985) trained black ministers as alcoholism counselors because "black ministers and black churches have traditionally served as core resources for their community's human services." (p. 183) In developing their program, they were particularly impressed by the fact that in a community survey of persons over 65 years of age none of the white respondents listed their local church a resource for help in alcohol related problems, but that 80% of the black respondents listed the church as such a resource. Because the minister is the focal point of the church community, Swift and Beverly theorized that by using black ministers as counselors, they could more effectively provide options for black offenders in the criminal justice system. While methodological problems made it impossible for firm conclusions to be drawn from their study, the basic success of the program was without doubt.

List of References

Allen, C. (1978). I'm Black & I'm Sober: A Minister's Daughter Tells Her Story About Fighting the Disease of Alcoholism-- and Winning. Minneapolis, Minnesota: CompCare Publications.

Artz, J. (1976). Can Minorities Be Invisible: If Not, Why Not? American Journal of Drug and Alcohol Abuse, 3(1), 181-83.

Bell, P., & Evans, J. (1981). Counseling the Black Client: Alcohol Use and Abuse in Black America. Center City, Minnesota: Hazelden.

Berlin, I. (1974). Slaves Without Masters: The Free Negro in the Antebellum South. New York, New York: Oxford University Press.

Brown, F., & Tooley, J. (May/June 1989). Alcoholism in the Black Community. The Counselor, 7(3), 35.

Caldwell, F. J. (1983). Alcoholics Anonymous as a Viable Treatment Resource for Black Alcoholics. in T. S. Watts, & R. Wright (eds.), Black Alcoholism: Toward a Comprehensive Understanding. (pp. 85-99). Springfield, Illinois: Charles C. Thomas.

Cayleff, S. E. (1986). Ethical Issues in Counseling Gender, Race, and Culturally Distinct Groups. Journal of Counseling and Development, 64(5), 345-347.

Douglas, F. (1892). Life and Times of Frederick Douglas. New York, New York: McMillan.

206

Dozier, C. D. (May/June 1989). The African-American and Alcoholism: Roadblocks to Treatment. The Counselor, 7(3), 33-34. Greene, L. J. (1969). The Negro in Colonial New England. New York, New York: Atheneum.

Hacker, G. (1987). Marketing Booze to Blacks: A Report from the Center for Science in the Public Interest. Washington, D.C.: Center for Science in the Public Interest.

Harding, V. (1981). There Is A River: The Black Struggle for Freedom in America. New York, New York: Harcourt Brace Jovanovich, Publishers.

Hudson, H. L. (1978 (unpublished). The History of Blacks and Alcoholics Anonymous. Doctoral dissertation, City University of New York, New York, New York.

Hudson, H. L. (1985-86). How and Why Alcoholics Anonymous Works for Blacks. Alcoholism Treatment Quarterly: Treatment of Black Alcoholics, 2(3/4), 11-30.

Icard, L., & Traunstein, D. M. (May, 1987). Black, Gay, Alcoholic Men: Their Character and Treatment. Social Casework, 267-272.

Jones, L. (1980). The Absence of the Black Professional and Semi-Professional in the Membership of Alcoholics Anonymous. in Inc. Association of Labor-Management Administrators. (pp. 416- 431). Arlinton, Virginia: ALMACA.

Lender, M. E., & Martin, J. K. (1982). Drinking in America: A History. New York, New York: The Free Press: A Division of Macmillan Publishing Co., Inc.

Levin, J. S. (1984). The Role of the Black Church in Community and Medicine. Journal of the National Medical Association, 76, 477-483.

Loewenberg, B. J. & R. Bogin (eds.), (1976). Black Women in Nineteenth-Century American Life: Their Words, Their Thoughts, Their Feelings. University Park, Pennsylvania: The Pennsylvania State University Press.

Miranda, M. & H. H. L. Kitano (eds.), (1986). Mental Health Research and Practice in Minority Communities: Development of Culturally Sensitive Training Programs. Rockville, Maryland: National Institute of Mental Health.

Mulford, H. A. (1970). From What to What -- And How? in D. L. Gatlin (ed.), Attitudes on Alcohol and Drugs. (pp. 6-7). North Conway, New Hampshire: Reporter Press.

Prugh, T. (1986/87). The Black Church: A Foundation for Recovery. Alcoholism Health and Research World, 11(2), 52,54.

Raboteau, A. J. (1978). Slave Religion: The "Invisible Institution" in the Antebellum South. New York, New York: Oxford University Press.

Ronan, L. (1986-87). Alcohol-Related Health Risks Among Black Americans. Alcohol Health and Research World, 11(2), 36-39, 65.

Schilling, B. (1986). Cross Cultural Counseling: A Guide for Nutrition and Health Counselors. Washington, D.C.: Department of Agriculture.

Swift, C., & Beverly, S. (1985). Utilization of Ministers as Alcohol Counselors and Educators: Increasing Prevention and Treatment Resources in the Black Community. in R. W., Thomas Wright (eds.), Prevention of Black Alcoholism. (pp. 182-198). Springfield, Illinois: Charles C. Thomas.

Thommie B. (1986). How Soon We Forget. Newsletters Anonymous, 1, 2.

Weems, R. (May, 1987). This Mother's Daughter. Essence, 75-76, 150, 152, 154.

Williams, Millree. (1982a). Alcoholism and Blacks: A Historical Context. Alcohol Health and Research World, 6(4), 33.

Williams, Millree. (1982b). Blacks and Alcoholism: Issues in the 80s. Alcohol Health and Research World, 6(4), 31-40.

This article was originally presented as a paper at the College Theology Society Conference, Rochester, NY, June, 1989. It is reprinted with permission of the authors.

THE BLACK CHURCH:
A FOUNDATION FOR RECOVERY

Thomas Prugh

In the African American community, the church is often a place of healing as well as worship. As a result, clergy can have a unique role in working with African American alcoholics.

In the words of a recent Government report, "Blacks appear to be at disproportionately high risk for certain alcohol-related health problems" (USDHHS 1985, p. 131). For example, according to research summarized in the DHHS report, the cirrhosis mortality rate among blacks is about twice that of nonminorities. Esophageal cancer, believed to be linked to alcohol consumption, occurs in black males at 10 times the rate that it occurs in white males. Although black teenagers apparently drink less and count fewer heavy drinkers among their number than do their white peers, high rates of heavy drinking and of alcohol-related social problems begin to surface among black males after the age of 30--several years after trends in these figures have begun to decline for white males. In general, the abuse of alcohol and other drugs is thought to be closely related to many of the causes of excess early mortality among black Americans (USDHHS 1985).

Neither the set of problems nor the concern is new. But the indifferent success of programs originally designed for white populations when applied in treating blacks (Swift and Beverly 1985) appears to have stimulated a search for additional resources to bring to bear on chemical abuse problems in the black community. As a result, more and more attention is being given to the potential of the clergy and the churches. It is pointed out that churches in the

United States are regularly in contact with at least 60 percent of the U.S. population (Gallup 1986) and that Americans consult clergy for help with personal problems more often than they consult any other professional group except physicians (Lieberman and Mullan, cited in Worthington 1986).

The Church as a Resource

These facts apply to Americans in general, but they may have special relevance for blacks because of the unique status of the churches in the black culture. "The churches are the only institutions 'owned' by blacks," declared Richard Green, Superintendent of Special School District #1 in Minneapolis, when addressing a recent conference on chemical dependence and the black community. Similarly, Levin (1984) wrote that the church is the only "autonomous social institution" in the black community and that it enjoys a unique status as "the seat of both worship and healing." It has traditionally ministered to a wide range of needs:

> The black church has been the conservator of the defining values and norms of black Americans. Black churches have served as houses of worship, schools, meeting places for fraternal organizations, and loci of community organization. The black minister has been teacher, preacher, funeral director, politician, and, recently, agent of health change. (p. 478)

The black church's strength as both spiritual refuge and agent of social change was perhaps never more apparent than during the civil rights movement of the 1960s and 1970s, when church-based groups helped sustain the movement and many of its most effective leaders came from the ranks of the clergy. The church's success in these roles lends credibility to the claim that it is "...the most profound instrument available to blacks when it comes to coping with the multiplicity of problems that beset their lives" (Knox 1985, p. 35). Furthermore, by sponsoring shared rituals that encourage group cohesion and that contribute to the participant's sense of identity, the church functions as a mental health resource (Knox, p. 37).

Major purposes of churches are, of course, to nurture and protect their members' spirituality and to encourage its expression. At the same time, this spirituality may thrive outside the structure of the churches: Many blacks who regard themselves as deeply spiritual belong to no church and seldom attend church services (Brisbane and Womble 1985; Knox 1985). In any case, this spirituality is often a powerful personal resource that can be tapped by clients struggling to cope with chemical abuse problems.

Not only is spirituality valuable in its own right, as a wellspring of hope and strength, but also a nonjudgmental openness to spiritual beliefs of clients can help persuade them to accept the kinds of help available through conventional treatment programs. This can make a crucial difference in those frequent cases of religious clients who fear that their values will be undermined by secular counseling (Worthington 1986).

Knox (1985), starting from the premise that "spirituality is deeply embedded in the black psyche," discusses the various expressions of spirituality and the ways it can be employed by therapists to help clients with alcohol problems.

Of particular interest is the belief in the church's power of salvation, which many black parents have instructed their children to rely on in time of trouble. Frances Larry Brisbane, Ph.D., professor of social work at the State University of New York at Stony Brook, suspects that this tradition may be weakening among younger blacks, who may no longer be attending church in the same numbers as their elders. But she argues that older blacks who retain their faith and connections with the church community often see the church as a practical and effective remedy for alcohol problems. Confronted with a troubled drinker, they may advise or even arrange for a return to the church, in the hope that roots will be rediscovered, a positive influence will be exerted, or even a healing "conversion" will be triggered.

A Task for the Clergy

What role does or should the clergy play? By most accounts, the role of the clergy is a central one, although the details are somewhat controversial. On the negative side, there is some evidence (Gallup 1986) that many of the clergy see alcoholism as a sin, a character flaw, or failure of willpower--a view that alcoholism professionals almost universally dispute and, indeed, find handicapping in dealing with alcohol abuse. In addition, the view of the nature of the self held by some members of the religious community as opposed to that held by the psychiatric and mental health communities can lead to mutual mistrust and alienation, to the ultimate detriment of clients (Knox 1985). This isolation of clergy from mental health professional appears to be most pronounced among conservative clergy, who also appear to contrast with their more liberal colleagues in the clergy in being more directive and less facilitative with clients (Worthington 1986).

On the other hand, Brisbane believes this to be both an inaccurate picture and a counterproductive one. It is often assumed, she argues, that ministers will be unwilling to address the problem, with the result that they are not even approached. Yet she knows of many members of the clergy who take an active role against alcohol problems. At least one study (Wright, cited in Knox 1985) also suggests that blacks widely approve of clergy who do so. Common sense dictates and research confirms that properly trained ministers can be effective as alcohol counselors and educators in the black community (see, for example, Swift and Beverly 1985). Brisbane's experience convinces her that drinkers seeking out a minister who understands alcoholism tend to prefer that kind of counseling to the services of formal treatment programs.

One minister who has taken an activist stance toward alcohol problems is the Reverend Lillian Webb, pastor of Mount Olive African Methodist Episcopal (AME) Church in Port Washington, NY. Webb believes that her training as a psychiatric social worker and her years of experience in drug and alcohol treatment programs have sensitized her to the problem and have prepared her for the role. She belongs to a denomination (the AME church) that is actively "working toward having some organizational, programmatic approach" to alcohol abuse and alcoholism. The AME church has accepted the disease model of alcoholism and has invited members of the National Black Alcoholism Council to past conferences in order to establish dialogue and to begin offering training opportunities to AME clergy.

The AME First Episcopal District (comprising the Mid- and North Atlantic Coastal States) has gone a step farther, by establishing a church-incorporated structure called Self-Help, Inc. (SHI). According to Webb, who chairs the organization, SHI is intended to be "a vehicle through which we can deal with some of the social ills that plague the black family," including (though not limited to) alcohol problems. Through SHI, the AME church hopes to develop resources to enable parishioners with alcohol problems to be referred for help within the church community; to provide training for clergy in alcohol concepts, counseling, and intervention skills; and perhaps to establish something like an employee assistance program for alcoholic clergy.

These examples suggest that the clergy as a group includes members who are acutely sensitive to the problems of alcohol abuse and who are aware of the need for action. Where others are less active, it may be because many of them feel inadequate to the task, owing partly to a lack of appropriate training (Gallup 1986). That training is available in all parts of the country, if not always from internal church sources such as Self-Help, Inc. It is found in external settings as diverse as locally sponsored workshops and nationally known summer schools for alcohol studies.

Beyond lectures and study, and beyond the need to be aware of local resources, Brisbane believes, the most important fact about alcoholism and alcohol problems needed by ministers is that whole families are affected--and those families may well be sitting in the congregation, even if the alcoholic member is not. Ministers can reach out to these parishioners, can take the lead in broaching the subject of alcoholism in the family: "Once they ask that question, they then release their parishioners to tell them the truth," Brisbane says. In so doing, in extending that hand, she says, the minister can help to fulfill the calling of the clergy and the mission of the church--to heal.

List of References

Brisbane, F.L., and Womble, M.   Treatment of Black Alcoholics. New York: The Haworth Press, 1985.

Gallup, G. A Plan to Bring the Clergy into the Alcoholism Battle. Alcoholism and Addiction 6 (3): 45, 1986.

Knox, D.H. Spirituality: A Tool in the Assessment and Treatment of Black Alcoholics and Their Families. In: Brisbane, F.L. and Womble, M. Treatment of Black Alcoholics. New York: The Haworth Press, 1985. pp. 31-44.

Levin, J.S. The Role of the Black Church in Community Medicine. Journal of the National Medical Association 76:477-483, 1984.

Minnesota Institute on Black Chemical Abuse. Chemical Dependency and Health in Black America. MIBCA Scope, Spring 1986, 1-2.

Swift, C.F. and Beverly, S. The Utilization of Ministers as Alcohol Counselors and Educators: Increasing Prevention and Treatment Resources in the Black Community. In: Wright, R. and Watts, T.D., eds. Prevention of Black Alcoholism: Issues and Strategies. Springfield, IL: Charles C. Thomas, 1985, pp. 182-198.

U.S. Department of Health and Human Services. Report of the Secretary's Task Force on Black and Minority Health: Volume I, Executive Summary. U.S. GPR #491-313/44706. Washington, D.C.: Supt. of Docs., U.S. Govt. Print. Off., 1985.

Worthington, E.L. Religious Counseling: A Review of
Published Empirical Research. <u>Journal of Counseling
and Development</u> 64: 421-431, 1986.

*This article originally appeared in <u>Alcohol Health and
Research World</u> 11.2 (1986/1987): 52-54. It is reprinted with
permission.*

For Further Reading on
Diversity Among Alcoholics

(January, 1989). Alcohol and Other Drug Use in Three Hispanic Populations: Mexican-Americans, Puerto Ricans, and Cuban-Americans. NCADI Update, 1-4.

This article describes the rate of drug use in three Hispanic communities.

(1975). Alcoholism in the Hispanic Community. Engage/Social Action, 3, 44-46.

In part, the article describes the services offered at the Sheridan Center which is located in the United Methodist Church.

Atkinson, D. R. (1987). Counseling Blacks: A Review of Relevant Research. Journal of College Student Personnel, 28(6), 552-558.

Atkinson reviews research which has been done concerning working with African-American clients.

Baker, J. (1977). Alcoholism and the American Indian. In N. J. Estes, &M. E. Heinemann (eds.), Alcoholism. (pp. 194-203). St. Louis: C.V. Mosby.

In this essay, Baker gives an historical background of alcohol use among Native Americans, the dynamics and nature of present day drinking, and trends in treatment. Religious and spiritual issues are mentioned throughout.

(1985). F. L. Brisbane, &M. Womble (eds.), Treatment of Black Alcoholics. New York, New York: Haworth Press.

The book includes essays on a variety of topics as they relate to African-American alcoholics and their families.

Brooks, B. (June, 1989). Moral Approach Fatal to Blacks. Michigan Alcohol and Addiction Association Dispatch, 12, 16.

Brooks argues that churches generally have a positive approach to alcohol education. He also claims that black ministers "make sincere efforts to help family members who have alcoholic parents or spouses" but that most admit they don't know what to do.

Brown, F., & Tooley, J. (1989). Alcoholism in the Black Community. The Counselor, 7(3), 35.

Brown and Tooley argue that "Black alcoholics are not a homogenous group," that "social class distinctions have been present throughout history: the degree of spirituality varies as well as self-esteem and racial pride."

Caetano, R. (1987). Acculturation and Attitudes Toward Appropriate Drinking Among U.S. Hispanics. Alcohol & Alcoholism, 22(4), 427-433.

Caetano found that respondents who were more acculturated had more liberal attitudes toward drinking.

Cayleff, S. E. (1986). Ethical Issues in Counseling Gender, Race, and Culturally Distinct Groups. Journal of Counseling and Development, 64(5), 345-347.

The article addresses the complex ethical and cultural issues that arise when counseling women, blacks, ethnic minorities, poor people, lesbians, and gays.

Christmas, J. J. (Spring, 1978). Alcoholism Services for Minorities: Training Issues and Concerns. Alcoholism Health and Research World, 20-27.

Christmas explains issues which surface when working with

minority clients. She emphasizes that the therapist must understand the client's culture.

Dozier, C. D. (1989). The African-American and Alcoholism: Roadblocks to Treatment. The Counselor, 7(3), 33-34.

Dozier argues that "If a counselor or agency is committed to treating African-American alcoholics and their families, then they must be willing to develop a culturally sensitive treatment program which must identify and address those issues which are unique to African-Americans." Some of those issues are explained in the article.

Dozier, E. P. (1966). Problem Drinking Among American Indians: The Role of Sociocultural Deprivation. Quarterly Journal of Studies on Alcohol, 27, 72-87.

Dozier provides background information on drinking practices, historical information, patterns of drinking, functions of drinking, and attempted solutions to the problem. Because drinking is viewed as an evil, traditional, non-Native American, and new religious movements have been used to combat excessive drinking. Special focus is placed on the New Religion of Hansome Lake.

Finnegan, D. G., & McNally, E. B. (1987). Dual Identities: Counseling Chemically Dependent Gay Men and Lesbians. Center City, Minnesota: Hazelden.

The first section of this book includes an excellent description of sexuality that is very readable. Section two raises specific issues which might be addressed in working with lesbian or gay clients.

Gaines, A. D. (1985). Alcohol: Cultural Conceptions and Social Behavior Among Urban Blacks. in L. A. Bennett, &G. M. Ames (eds.), American Experience with Alcohol. (pp. 171-197). New York, New York: Plenum Press.

Gaines investigates folk beliefs which blacks have concerning alcohol.

Garcia, S. D., &Panagoulias, P. (eds.) (1983). Drink the Winds, Let the Waters Flow Free. Minneapolis: Johnson Institute.

A collection of historical and contemporary prayers, meditations, and personal testimonials about alcohol recovery in the Native American Tradition

Isobel, W., Sr. Florence, Anita N., & Evelyn T. (1971). Women Can be Alcoholics. NCCA Blue Book, 23, 58-70.

In this panel discussion, each woman tells the story of her addiction and recovery.

Jeanne E. (1987). Women and Spirituality. Center City, MN: Hazelden.

Jeanne describes some of the special issues which face some women in accepting a higher power. The booklet ends with five testimonials from women who describe the higher powers in their lives.

Jilek-Aall, L. (1981). Acculturation, Alcoholism and Indian Style Alcoholics Anonymous. Journal of Studies on Alcohol, Supplement 9, 143-158.

Jilek-aall gives a history of alcohol use by native Americans and describes various methods used to help alcoholics. He then gives an analysis of how AA was introduced and developed among the coast Salish Indians.

Kirpatrick, J. (1978). Turnabout: Help for a New Life. Garden City, NY: Doubleday.

The first section of this book is Kirkpatrick's story of her alcoholism and recovery. The second section outlines the steps of Women for Sobriety.

Kus, R. J. (1989). Bibliotherapy and Gay American Men of Alcoholics Anonymous. Journal of Gay and Lesbian Psychotherapy, 1(2), 73-86.

Kus explains how reading is used by gay men to grow spiritually as they recover from alcoholism and other drug addiction. Positive and negative aspects of bibliotherapy are explained.

Loan, C. (1989). Cross Cultural Awareness: A First Step. The Counselor, 7(3), 19-20.

Loan argues that "Effective counselors must balance their mastery of counseling techniques with a sensitivity to the cultural grounding of their clients.

Maddahian, E. (1988). Risk Factors for Substance Use: Ethnic Differences Among Adolescents. Journal of Substance Abuse, 1, 11- 23.

The authors study the risk factors for black, Asian, Hispanic, and white adolescents.

Nugent, J. A. (1984). Ministry to the Most Abandoned. NCCA Blue Book, 36, #14.

Nugent tells about the problem of alcoholism in his predominantly black parish. He describes the problems the homeless face in getting treatment and about founding "Our Father's House," a 90- day half-way house.

(1987). A Personal Look at AIDS and Recovery. NALGAP News, 8(4), 2,5.

This anonymous gay man reflects on how AIDS has affected his AA program. Special emphasis is placed on how he thanks God for permitting him to enjoy the day. Sponsorship, medication for pain, and resentments are emphasized.

Ronan, L. (1986-87). Alcohol-Related Health Risks Among Black Americans. Alcohol Health and Research World, 11(2), 36-39, 65.

"This article summarizes some of the data compiled during the [Black and Minority Health] task force's investigation into the role that alcohol plays in contributing to the health disparity between black and white Americans.

Swallow, J. (ed.) (1983). Out From Under: Sober Dykes and Our Friends. San Francisco: Spinsters Ink.

The book includes poems, fiction, and interviews with lesbians who have recovered from alcoholism.

ALCOHOLIC CLERGY AND
WOMEN RELIGIOUS

ALCOHOLIC PRIESTS:
ARE THEY EFFECTIVE PASTORS?

Steven L. Berg

Because alcoholics are frequently known for their character defects, it seems unlikely that an alcoholic could make a competent priest. However, participating in Alcoholics Anonymous brings spiritual renewal. When thinking of alcoholic clergy, it is important to remember that recovery is possible and that nuns, seminarians, deacons, and rabbis, like priests, can return to full, effective ministry.

In two separate articles, Dean Marr has claimed that alcoholics make better pastors.[1] A similar attitude can be found in Bishop Michael Dempsey's observation that "Some of the greatest priests in America are priests who have had an alcoholic problem."[2] On the surface, such a position seems foolish.

David Stewart claims that the alcoholic is childish, overly sensitive, grandiose, impulsive, intolerant, and given to

---

[1]Dean Marr, "Alcoholics Can Make Better Pastors," Catholic Digest 44.10 (1980)82-85 and "Why Alcoholics Make Better Pastors" Today's Parish (May/June 1980).

[2]Michael Dempsey, "Address of Welcome," NCCA Blue Book 21 (1969) 2.

wishful thinking.[3]   One author warns that alcoholics can rationalize lusty sexual excursions into romance, that they too often enjoy gossip barbed with anger; have feelings of superiority, envy, righteousness, gluttony, and sloth which they describe with less harsh words; and that they waste time wishing for what they don't have rather than working for it.[4] And another author has gone so far as to describe the alcoholic personality as devilish, hardly a characteristic that is welcomed for priestly candidates.[5] Yet Dean Marr and Bishop Dempsey would not only welcome these alcoholic men into the ministry but also claim that they have superior talents as pastors.

Irony of Claim

The irony of such a claim comes from the fact that Mr. Marr, Bishop Dempsey, and others who recognize the gifts which alcoholic priests bring to the ministry are not referring to the alcoholic who is still drinking. Instead, they are talking about recovered alcoholic priests, men whose alcoholism visited upon them the trials of Job and who, like Job, survived with a strengthened spiritual base. They are men who "were great priests before they had the problem

---

[3]David A. Stewart, "Empathy in the Group Therapy of Alcoholics," Quarterly Journal of Studies on Alcohol 15 (1954) 74-110.

[4]Twelve Steps and Twelve Traditions, (New York: AA World Services, 1952) 66-67.

[5]Our Devilish Alcoholic Personalities, Center City, MN: Hazelden, 1975.

and often it was their dedication to their ministry, their hours of untiring service that brought on the problem."[6]

But what does the alcoholic priest do that is so valuable? From materials compiled at Guest House, we know that Fr. James worked with the missions in Chile, that Fr. Vince wrote a book on counseling and that Fr. Georges wrote one on the Soviet Union, that Fr. William has a special ministry with minority groups, that Fr. James' ministry is educating youth, and that Fr. Jim helps the deaf hear the promise of God's blessing. Some priests such as Fr. Joe and Fr. Vaughan work in treatment facilities, and others like Fr. Francis, conduct seminars for seminarians so they too can be more effective pastors.[7] Besides the fact that they are all effective priests, the one thing that these men have in common is their involvement with Alcoholics Anonymous.

Before addressing the issue of AA involvement, it is important to realize that alcoholism is a three fold malady: physical, mental, and spiritual. Physical affects of alcoholic drinking such as a destroyed liver are easy to measure. Grandiose thinking and rationalizations are examples of the types of mental problems which alcoholics have. As their drinking progresses they find it more and more difficult to function in the world because they don't think and react like

---

[6]Bishop Dempsey, 2.

[7]The stories of these priests and many more are found in Guest House, a quarterly publication of Guest House, an in-patient treatment facility for alcoholic priests, brothers, and seminarians. The information recorded here is compiled from the following issues of this newsletter: September 1970, September 1974, 8.3 (1977), 9.1 (1978), 9.2 (1978), 11.2 (1980), 15.2 (1984), and 17.1 (1986).

other people. Although they might not be certifiably mentally ill, in many ways they live in a fantasy world.

Isolated from God

While describing the spiritual effects of alcoholism, Paul V. Sullivan argues that "the person involved in the throes of alcoholism is in every sense alone." This sense of aloneness is caused by a separation not only from other human beings, but also from God. As Sullivan explains, the alcoholic "isolates himself from God even though he may still believe in God."[8] Even priests can isolate themselves from the God to whom they have dedicated their lives if they do not practice a life of spiritual renewal. And a lack of attention paid to spirituality is characteristic of alcoholics.

Because alcoholism causes spiritual and mental as well as physical decline, contented sobriety does not result by the simple act of not drinking. While the first step to recovery comes from not drinking, the character defects which are associated with alcoholics continue unless spirituality is addressed. As Fr. Mark Mindrup explains, spiritual renewal is needed both in terms of religious development but also in terms of recovery from alcoholism.[9]

Priests have found that AA brings spiritual renewal. After making the decision not to drink, priests--like all others who suffer from alcoholism--are welcomed into the AA program. In fact, admission of powerlessness over

---

[8]Paul V. Sullivan, "The Spiritual Effects of Alcoholism," <u>NCCA Blue Book</u> 25 (1973) 33.

[9]Mark Mindrup, "Renewal," <u>NCCA Blue Book</u> 28 (1976) 120-125.

alcohol and recognition that life has become unmanageable is the first step of AA's twelve step recovery program. And it is the only step that specifically mentions alcohol. The remaining steps concern themselves with spiritual renewal.

After taking the first step of recovery, the priest who enters AA is asked to turn his will and his life over to the care of the God he understands. In effect, he is asked to end his isolation from God. As he reacquaints himself with his higher power, the priest takes a moral inventory which he shares with another person. Edward C. Sellner is just one of the many people who have compared this step to the sacrament of reconciliation.[10]

Following the inventory, AA-alcoholic's ask God to remove their defects as they go about the process of making amends for the harm that they had done.

Suited for Priests

Francis J. Crotty, in an article on the "Basics of Recovery," argues that recovery, like the disease of alcoholism, is progressive, that recovery is a process.[11]

And like all other processes, recovery takes time. As the alcoholic priest works the program advocated by Alcoholics Anonymous, he enters into a recovery process. While there are other recovery programs available, AA is especially suited for the priest because of its spiritual basis. It is for

---

[10]Edward C. Sellner, Christian Ministry and the Fifth Step. Center City, MN: Hazelden, 1981.

[11]Francis J. Crotty, "Basics of Recovery," NCCA Blue Book 30 (1978) 260-267.

this reason that individuals working to help alcoholic priests have historically recommended the AA program.[12]

Because AA does not advocate any particular spiritual program, AA meetings rarely address specific spiritual issues. But the recovering priest is able to find spiritual renewal with other Catholics if he becomes involved in Calix, a group of Catholics who have recovered through AA. In Calix, the priest is able to work with others who understand and have a strong commitment to Catholicism.

Skills Recognized?

Recovered alcoholic priests approach their ministry with a continued sense of spiritual renewal. But when they return to their work in parishes or prisons or missions or where ever their talents take them, recovered alcoholic priests are not the same great priests whom Bishop Dempsey described. They are better. While they continue to be dedicated to their ministry, their recovery program in Alcoholics Anonymous helps prevent them from acting on the unhealthy character traits which lead to their eventual isolation from God and community.

But are the recovered priest's skills recognized by his parishioners? A brief anecdote by Fr. William J. Clausen answers this question in the affirmative. Clausen, a recovered alcoholic, was being transferred to another parish, a move he mentioned to a teenager in the parish he was

---

[12]"Panel of People Who Work with Alcoholics," NCCA Blue Book 20 (1968) 64-83. Although this article is 20 years old, it still reflects the prevailing attitude in the field of recovery.

leaving. He explains that he was surprised at the teenager's reaction.

> "Is the Bishop sending us another alchy priest?" he asked.
> "No, my successor is not an alcoholic."
> "Aw, nuts!" he shot back.[13]

While it would be foolish to argue that priests who have not suffered the effects of alcoholism are somehow inferior to alcoholic priests, Dean Marr's observation is essentially correct. "When alcoholics truly recover in AA, they develop a marvelous sense of balance. They learn to love again because they have lifted from them the thing that blinds them to themselves."[14] After experiencing the spiritual renewal that is unavoidable in AA, the recovered alcoholic priest should be sought after by Bishops and requested by parishioners because, as recovery progresses they only become better.

This article originally appeared in the August, 1989 issue of *The Priest* *and is reprinted with permission.*

---

[13]William J. Clausen, "Homily--June 17, 1986," NCCA Blue Book 38 (1986) 127.

[14]Joseph C. Martin, "Learn to Love Again," Guest House 17.2 (1986) 9.

ALCOHOL AND OTHER DRUGS IN SPIRITUAL FORMATION

*Alcohol and other drugs do play a role
in spiritual development. Sometimes
this role is negligible. At other times it
is extremely destructive. However, with
proper intervention, the alcoholic can
recover and live life of spiritual growth.*

"The only alcohol problem I ever had in the seminary was where could I get my next drink." This recollection of a recovered alcoholic priest recounting his story is probably typical of more young religious and seminarians than is realized. Alcohol and other drugs, especially prescription rather than street drugs, are simply a part of our society today. Unless there is a serious problem, the tendency is to take them for granted and certainly not see them as a threat to spiritual formation (Ford, 1959).

Wine at dinner is no longer only for big feasts in the convent, and beer is presumed to be a harmless source of conviviality. Neither is recognized as having the same alcohol as hard liquor, and as having the danger of addiction. Alcohol in some form is considered a necessity for any picnic or social gathering, male or female. Our good Catholic doctors prescribe tranquilizers and sleeping pills on the naive presumption that no sister or priest could possibly be a "junkie" or addict. Perhaps more important is the fact often missed that, short of alcoholism or other addictions, even "moderate" use of these substances can interfere notably with the development of a vigorous spiritual life.

The facts, of course, contradict some implicit assumptions in all the above. The percentage of alcoholism and other addictions among priests and religious is now being reported as probably higher than in the average population (NCCA), and higher than reported earlier (Fichter, 1977; Sorenson, 1976). It often goes on longer undetected, or even if suspected goes on longer before it is confronted by superiors or there is an intervention by concerned peers. I know one sister who was getting pills from five different doctors, another who shopped the various liquor stores telling the clerk in each that there was a special feast coming up, a priest who drank himself to death while his brother priests covered his weddings and funerals for him, a sacristan who consumed large quantities of altar wine without being suspected, and one alcoholic nun who was put into treatment whereupon the prioress found 68 bottles of pills in her room.

This last case illustrates the fact of polydrug or cross-addiction, which is extremely damaging to the body because the effects of alcohol and other drugs in the system do not just add: they multiply, in what is called potentation or synergism. Polydrug use is so common now that we train our alcoholism counselors not to ask **whether** one is using drugs, but to routinely ask "and **what** other drugs are you using?" If the assumption is wrong, it will be corrected and no harm is done.

But, you say, they know better. Of course. Doctors, nurses and dentists know more about drugs than most people, and they have an above-average incidence of problems. Dr. Claudia Black's book on the children of alcoholics has the poignant but terrifying title, "**It Will Never Happen to Me**" (1981) which tells of the millions of youngsters who become alcoholics in spite of resolving never to touch the stuff because of what they see it did to their parents. Knowledge does not guarantee conduct: I **know** how to shoot par golf, but that doesn't mean I do it--any more than being a professional psychologist guarantees my being perfectly adjusted.

Causality

How does all this get started? Very subtly. Contrary to the now outmoded theory that alcoholism is the symptom of some underlying personality problem which the victim is trying to sedate, it is now recognized that alcoholics are mostly normal people who start drinking for the same reasons as everybody else: to be sociable, to relax, out of custom. The problem is that about one out of ten becomes addicted to the drug. All too often the addiction is seen as the result or symptom of psychological problems, instead of the cause of them, as is the usual case.

Many, but not all, of these have a hereditary biological disposition, which may not appear in their parents but might be traced back to a grandparent who lived and died before alcoholism was recognized as a disease. Hence the importance of good screening and education. Not that those with a history of alcoholism in their ancestry should be denied a vocation: just that "forewarned is forearmed" here; they should know that they are biologically more vulnerable and that total abstinence might be the wiser or even a necessary route for them.

I recently met a sister who had been an alcoholic since age 14, entered the sisterhood at 22, and shortly thereafter as a novice was admitted to an alcoholism treatment center. A liver scan showed the effects of her heavy teen-age drinking, but how many physicians will routinely run a liver scan on a sister applicant? In early years of seminary or religious life, diagnosis and especially early detection can be quite difficult. The physician is reluctant to suspect alcoholism or other drug abuse. Those in charge of formation tend to dismiss the symptoms as immaturity or rebellion which will disappear in time.

They don't disappear in time, so the person is shunted from one assignment to another instead of being confronted with the real problem. Confrontation is difficult, and always mixed with a fear that one will lose a friend, or at least get the subject angry. But Christian fortitude here is also genuine charity, now often called "tough love." The fear that one will lose a friend is counteracted by the statement of a director at Guest House that when recovered priests return to their diocese after treatment for alcoholism and other addictions, they are most grateful to those who forced them into treatment. The ones they are angry at are their peers who encouraged them to be "one of the boys" when they were progressing in a terminal illness.

Diagnosis

The fact that the sister in the polydrug case cited above also had a Master's degree and a very responsible administrative position parallels the fact that it is often the most capable priests and religious who develop these problems, and go longest without suspicion because they are respected and trusted. Since it is a disease of denial, a classic symptom of alcoholism is the assertion, "I can quit any time I want to" or "I can take it or leave it alone." (The true social drinker doesn't have to play these games of control, or make these protestations.) But a superior wants to trust the subject, and often believes a con line that no experienced alcoholism counselor would buy for a minute. Again, good tolerance is mistakenly thought to be a sign that things are under control, that one can "handle" one's liquor, whereas the truth is that high tolerance tells us they are alcoholics.

Drinking more than one intends, short of getting drunk, is a sign often missed by those who still have the false stereotype of an alcoholic as one who always gets drunk every time they drink. In this case praying over it, or retreat resolutions about cutting down, may be just pious bargaining games one is playing with God to avoid the complete surrender implied in a frank admission that one is alcoholic and cannot drink moderately.

One diagnostic tool is to make a check list of all of the person's life problems with no reference to alcohol, then go back and see how many of these problems are alcohol-related in fact. The next step is to get an accurate account of the number of prescriptions that have been written for the person in the last five years, and all other sources of drugs of all kinds. The result can be amazing, and easily reveal the major root of what seemed to be other problems.

An honest drinking history is not easy to obtain, as alcoholics are notorious for deceiving both themselves and others. Vague, evasive answers like "not very much" and "sometimes not at all" are suspect. They don't count how much they had, and sometimes honestly do not remember-- a blackout does not mean passing out but amnesia later on even though one is quite conscious at the time. Thinking about drinking, or planning one's next drink, is typical of alcoholics. So is giving reasons (excuses) for drinking, or using alcohol to cope rather than merely enjoying it. Here are some symptoms that can add up even though any one by itself is not conclusive: procrastination on assignments and lack of punctuality for meetings or tasks, undependability often combined with blaming others, personality change or moodiness, irritability, secretiveness, careless dress and appearance, heavy use of breath mints and mouth wash, unaccountable expenditures, and avoidance of old friends.

Physical symptoms of alcohol and other drug misuse may appear only in later stages: pupils of eyes contracted or dilated, use of sun-glasses when not in sun, glazed "spaced-out" look in eyes, sweaty palms, slight hand tremor, morning cough, high blood pressure, puffiness or redness or small veins on nose or chin, acid stomach (frequent use of Tums, Rolaids), skin disorders, or trouble fighting off infections and colds. Sleep disturbances, fatigue, nervousness, digestive system disorders, headaches, heavy smoking and coffee consumption are all suggestive of alcohol or other drug problems.

Spiritual "Disease"

Addiction is now recognized as a disease (AMA, 1984). But unlike many illnesses it is not just physical, nor the province solely of the medical profession. It is a physical, psychological, social and spiritual disease. Let us examine what we mean by saying it is a spiritual disease.

Health is integral functioning, the whole person being able to relate to the whole of reality in proper proportion. Sickness or disease is a defect in this integral functioning, a lack-of-ease or dysfunction. Alcohol and other drugs impair one's ability to think and feel right about God, to function in relation to God as one should. The result is spiritual disease. One cannot be comfortable in the presence of the Creator, gets distorted ideas of God or feelings toward God which make it difficult to really trust and love. One is ill-at-ease with God, not attuned to the Infinite which is the most important part of the whole of reality to which one must relate. Alcohol or marijuana or pills anesthetize one's sensitivity to spiritual values. Religion becomes sick: mechanical, shallow, external instead of deeply felt and experienced. Spiritual life becomes dormant, but one is anesthetized to that fact, too.

One can be very active in a religion with a low level of spiritual life, or be very spiritual without even belonging to a religion. Gordon Allport of Harvard probably was getting at this distinction between religious and spiritual when he researched external vs. internal religion. The distinction is often used to explain why Alcoholics Anonymous is not a religion, although it is an intensely spiritual program and its Twelve Steps are centered around God, with alcohol being mentioned only once. The result is that AA can be a boost to the religious life of anyone, regardless of their religion. It is very concerned with spiritual health, because it recognizes alcoholism as being also a spiritual disease as well as physiological and psychological.

Deterioration of the person's spiritual life is almost inevitable as addiction to alcohol or other drugs starts to progress. Subtle at first, and not related in the mind of either the person or their spiritual advisor, the connection is often realized only during recovery. It is hard to pray well when one is high, or hung over. Eventually prayer becomes a mere formality, though it rarely ceases altogether in a priest or religious. Sometimes it takes the form of prayer asking God to remove the alcohol/drug problem, but it is never thoroughgoing and effective because, as mentioned above, there is no real surrender to the fact of addiction at this point.

I think it useful, and tactful, for those of us who are not alcoholics to refrain from describing how an alcoholic feels (Royce, 1984). Rather than telling them that all alcoholics are liars, say "alcoholics tell me they have problems with telling the truth." How do alcoholics describe themselves? As feeling discouraged, powerless, guilty, frustrated at their lack of will power, anxious, dishonest, self-centered, alienated from God and the community, with low frustration tolerance, lacking true humility but with low self-esteem. They are indeed spiritually sick (Royce, 1981, chapter 18).

They may also report some moral deterioration. At one time this was thought to be the cause of alcoholism, which was looked upon as moral depravity or weak will. We now know that this is the result, not the cause, of the addiction. They may have become dishonest, selfish, neglectful of duties to the point of at least some sins of omission. Their guilt feelings may be grossly exaggerated, and they need to be reassured that they are sick, not bad. In any case they are probably discouraged, depressed. They need to know that this is **their** dark night of the soul, that emptying of the cup of all that is material before it can be filled with God.

Prevention

Much of this describes later stages of the illness. During the formative years this may all be quite minimal, and imperceptible to the average spiritual guide or superior. But it is happening, in seminaries and in religious orders of women and men all over. It is indeed very difficult to separate the mere fun and partying from the early stages of addiction. Superiors are loathe to be suspicious, but the fact is that Jansenism and Prohibition have had the pendulum effect of swinging us too far in the opposite direction. It is only partly in jest that I speculate as to how many Catholics, during the Prohibition years and the century of bitter emotional battles which led up to it, drank themselves into alcoholism to prove they were not Methodists or Baptists.

Let's look at the facts. An estimated 16% of American priests have their apostolic effectiveness impeded to some degree by alcohol. Note that we do not say they are all full-blown alcoholics. But the work of God should not be diminished even to that degree by an avoidable cause. And most of it could be avoided if the seeds were detected early in formation. Not that dire threats and warnings by themselves are effective prevention. Not even good education alone can accomplish that. But education is the first phase of prevention. It is appalling the amount of ignorance one observes in supposedly sophisticated and educated people when it comes to the facts about alcohol and other drugs.

The current interest among the young in nutrition and good health habits, the whole human potential movement, can be capitalized on in prevention efforts. Alcohol is the classic case of "empty calories" - 210 calories to the ounce with no protein, no vitamins, no minerals. It attacks every organ and tissue in the human body, especially the brain and liver. It should be stressed that alcohol causes more problems than alcoholism. One does not have to be an alcoholic to kill somebody with an automobile after drinking even moderate amounts. Nor does one have to be an identifiable alcoholic to have their spiritual growth stunted by drinking. Our description of spiritual disease given above could apply to many seminarians and religious in formation long before they are recognized as alcoholics.

Besides education, the next prevention need is a psychological climate in our houses of formation which does not look down on abstinence as prissy or old-fashioned. I am not a total abstainer nor a recovered alcoholic; but we need to admit that temperance is, after all, one of the Christian virtues we are supposed to be inculcating in our young charges. It is irony that there are 37 million ex-smokers in the U.S., and the heir to the R.J. Reynolds tobacco fortune came out in the Spring of 1986 as publicly opposing cigarettes, while professed pursuers of an ascetical life and even many of their spiritual directors are still puffing away. Nicotine is an extremely addictive drug. Smoking is an expensive habit not in accord with the Christian poverty we pretend to advocate when we talk about concern for the poor, nor with the mortification proper to followers of the Christ who said that unless we take up our cross we are not worthy to be called his disciples. Yet smokers are treated as privileged members of the community in many religious houses. And any attempt to restrict alcohol consumption is looked upon as priggish.

What I propose is not Prohibition. It is not a high level of sanctity. It is very low-level asceticism, if you will, the minimum one might reasonably expect of people who claim to be pursuing Christian perfection. It is just common-sense care of one's health, a moral obligation we all have. We cannot perpetuate the attitudes of the past which grew out of ignorance of the effects of alcohol and other drugs on the human body. The Reynolds heir explained his stand to the press by saying that when his grandfather built up his tobacco fortune it was not known what we know today about the impact of smoking on health. Perhaps the tendency toward rebellion and protest which are characteristic of youth may be useful here. Young people may take rightful satisfaction in rejecting the stupidity of their elders in these matters.

Community attitudes can be changed, and indeed are changing in America with regard to smoking and drunk driving. Heavy drinking is no longer looked upon as a sign of sophistication or manliness. Pushing drinks, instead of being seen as generous hospitality, is now viewed as dangerous and the possible source of a civil liability lawsuit. Drunken behavior is no longer considered funny. One wonders why clergy and religious are not in the forefront of such changes instead of dragging their feet.

Thirdly, plenty of alternatives, attractive and readily available, should always accompany alcoholic beverages any time they are served. One should have a choice, and I don't mean between Scotch and Bourbon. At one university, the Friday night keggers dropped from eight kegs of beer to five per night, without any rules or moralizing, when the student body leaders decided to have plenty of their favorite soft drinks available, ice cold and very prominently displayed. Many students would switch to soft drinks after one or two beers or say, "I prefer 7-Up [or Pepsi] tonight." The whole lifestyle in a seminary or religious house should avoid the implication that alcohol is necessary to have fun or to socialize.

Fourthly, spiritual directors need to be alert to the connection between the problems presented to them and possible misuse of alcohol and other drugs. Anger, for instance, is often the result of being frustrated, hurt, irritated in ways that we all suffer. But alcohol can keep one from learning more constructive and Christian ways of dealing with anger, and indeed may be the cause of hurt or frustration in the first place. Anxiety is a typical excuse for drinking, yet the net effect of alcohol is to make one more anxious, similarly with trying to cope with depression by drinking alcohol, which is itself a depressant. Inability to get along with others and general alienation (except from drinking companions) can be an early warning sign of future addiction.

Ego problems betray a genuine humility, the most fundamental and the most difficult virtue in the spiritual life. Low self-esteem is a perennial problem, often accompanied by anxiety and depression. The rejection and failure, real or imagined, which stem from feelings of low self-worth are often the result of drinking and in turn are used as an excuse for more drinking in a vicious cycle of self-defeat.

Guilt naturally ensues, and the resulting feelings of unworthiness and self-blame can seriously interfere with any solid spiritual growth. Indecisiveness may be related to the anesthetizing effect of drugs, including alcohol, on one's ability to think through alternatives and make clearcut decisions.

Spiritual Recovery

Rather than an obstacle to spiritual growth or even a tragedy, addiction can be a great boost to one's spiritual life. As mentioned earlier, Alcoholics Anonymous is a beautiful and psychologically sound spiritual program, which can enhance the life of grace in anyone who practices the twelve steps. Several professional psychologists, for example Dr. Brown (1985), have shown how AA, and psychotherapy can be quite compatible. And certainly the AA literature contains a wealth of helps for spiritual growth. Apthorp (1985) has given us a clergy manual which demonstrates in detail how AA principles can be used in parish work. Robin Norwood, in her book Women Who Love Too Much (1985), showing how the twelve steps can be applied to other obsessive-compulsive tendencies, emphasizes the spiritual dimensions of the steps. All this can be integrated readily with Catholic spirituality. Although not a member, I go to open meetings of AA because it is good for my spiritual life. One pair of sisters who are AA and Al-Anon, respectively, do a great deal of good with their talks to both religious and laity.

It is true that AA is not the only or necessary way to sobriety, but good sociological research (Fichter, 1982) confirms what common sense would suspect, namely that the highest percentage of successful recovery in alcoholic priests occurs when they attend AA regularly after discharge from treatment. Today seminarians and novices are getting into AA long before in-patient treatment would be necessary. What they are surprised to find is that any AA group will welcome a sister or priest or seminarian without the slightest condescension and nary a raised eyebrow. Instead, what one hears at AA meetings is St. Augustine's, "there but for the grace of God go I."

Of course, one goes to AA meetings in mufti and is there to listen and profit, not counsel or preach. And if one has a polydrug problem, tact and discretion suggest that one concentrate on the alcohol problem and not bring up the other drugs if that is offensive to the group. (The same is true of using Antabuse, which is quite compatible with AA and has saved many lives; but some AA's mistakenly object, and its use is often better left unmentioned.) However, mention of polydrug abuse, provided alcohol is a principal drug, is now becoming very common at many AA meetings and is actually encouraged in an AA Conference-approved pamphlet (1978, p.16).

Many alcoholic priests and religious have reported that compared to what they learned in AA, their whole previous spiritual life was shallow, and their relation to God was very impersonal. Resignation to God's will becomes a reality in their use of Steps Three and Six/Seven (see Chapter 5, "How It Works," in the book **Alcoholics Anonymous**, 1939, 1976). They use the word **surrender**, although I prefer **acceptance**. "Thy will be done" becomes a reality in their life. The whole "Our Father" takes on a richer meaning than they ever imagined.

They have really learned how to pray and meditate by practicing Step Eleven: "sought by prayer and meditation to improve our conscious contact with God as we understood Him, seeking only a knowledge of His will and the power to carry that out." This can be rather a high-level spirituality:

seeking **only** God's will!   Their concept of God is transformed from that of a punishing tyrant to that of a loving, wise, and kind parent. They can truly pray to God as "Abba" with all the familiarity of **Mamma** or **Daddy** implied by this term.

And from a feeling of helplessness they grow into a realization with St. Paul that "I can do all things in Him who strengthens me." They learn that it is good theology to say God helps those who help themselves. Like a good Al-Anon, God is not a Rescuer or Enabler. Turning one's life and will over to the care of God does not mean sitting back and letting God do it. We must still produce, but under the care of a loving God.

They learn that confession is more than "dumping garbage" and that forgiveness is not analysis of why one did something, to explain it away. Reconciliation means healing, spiritual health, re-establishing a personal relationship with God, getting "at ease" with Him again. True humility means being comfortable with our human imperfection, a recognition of the truth that we are not bad but just **not-God**, to use the phrase from the title of Kurtz's (1979) definitive scholarly history of AA whose theme is that it is the history of over a million people who discovered that they are not God. They learn that AA claims spiritual progress, not perfection.

Sobriety is more than just abstinence. Merely avoiding a drink is a pretty empty way of life. AA's live life to the full, joyfully and with a clean conscience, with plenty of fun and no hangovers. I am often asked why I work in this field, to which the answer is simple: it is a source of great satisfaction to see recovering alcoholics get well, start to look better and feel better, grow spiritually and in their zest for life. They become not only well but "weller than well"--which now seems to be confirmed by research using psychological tests (Mellor et al., 1986). This is not meant in any "healthier than thou" sense, but at least to the extent that they are better off than they would have been had they never been alcoholics and hence never discovered how much God loves them and how much they love God.

Although there are no rules, most identify themselves at AA meetings with "My name is Mary [or Joe] and I am a GRATEFUL alcoholic" which reminds us that St. Ignatius of Loyola and many other great mystics tell us that the beginning of the love of God is gratitude for his gifts. And there are none more thankful than recovered alcoholics. Married lovers tell me that after intercourse they sometimes just murmur "Thank you, thank you, thank you..." and that might well be the prayer of one who loves God very much.

References

Alcoholics Anonymous, <u>Alcoholics Anonymous: The Story of How Many Thousands of Men and Women Have Recovered from Alcoholism</u>. New York: AA World Services, 1939; 3rd ed. 1976.

Alcoholics Anonymous, "A Clergyman Looks at AA." New York: AA World Services, 1961.

Alcoholics Anonymous, "The AA Member and Drug Abuse." New York: AA World Services, rev. 1978.

<u>Alcoholism: An Inherited Disease</u>. Washington, D.C.: National Institute on Alcohol Abuse and Alcoholism, 1985.

AMA, <u>Journal of the American Medical Association</u>, Oct. 12, 1984, vol. 252, no. 14 (entire issue).

246

Apthorp, Stephen P., <u>Alcohol and Substance Abuse</u>. Wilton, CT: Morehouse-Barlow, 1985.

Black, Claudia, <u>It Will Never Happen to Me</u>! Denver: Medical Administration Co.,1981.

Brown, Stephanie, <u>Treating the Alcoholic: A Developmental Theory of Recovery</u>. New York: Wiley, 1985.

Clinebell, Howard J., <u>Understanding and Counseling the Alcoholic Through Religion and Psychology</u>. Nashville: Abingdon Press, rev. 1968.

Fichter, Jos. H., "Alcohol and Addiction: Priests and Prelates," <u>America</u>, Oct. 22, 1977, 137:258-260.

Fichter, Jos. H., <u>The Rehabilitation of Clergy Alcoholics</u>. New York: Human Sciences Press, 1982. [Reviewed in <u>America</u>, Mar. 27, 1982, 142:244.]

Ford, John C., S.J., "Chemical Comfort and Christian Virtue," <u>American Ecclesiastical Review</u>, 1959, 141 (6):361-379.

Kurtz, Ernest, <u>Not-God: A History of Alcoholics Anonymous</u>. Center City, MN: Hazelden, 1979.

Kurtz, Ernest, "Why AA Works: The Intellectual Significance of Alcoholics Anonymous," <u>Journal of Studies on Alcohol</u>, 1982, 43:38-80.

Mellor, Steven, et al., "Comparative Trait Analysis of Long-term Recovering Alcoholics," Psychological Reports, 1986, 58: 411-418.

National Clergy Council on Alcoholism, The Blue Book. NCCA, 1200 Varnum St. N.E., Washington, D.C. 20017-2796, yearly.

Norwood, Robin, Women Who Love Too Much. Los Angeles: Jeremy P. Tarcher, Inc., 1985.

Royce, James E., Alcohol Problems and Alcoholism. New York: Free Press/Macmillan, 1981.

Royce, James E., "Inside the Alcoholic," Voices: The Art and Science of Psychotherapy, Spring, 1984, 20 (1): 21-25.

Royce, James E., "Alcoholism and Other Drug Dependencies," in R.J. Wicks et al. (eds), Clinical Handbook of Pastoral Counseling, pp. 502-519. New York: Paulist Press, 1985.

Sorenson, Andrew A., Alcoholic Priests: A Sociological Study. New York: Seabury Press, 1976.

This article originally appeared in Studies in Formative Spirituality 6.2 (1987): 211-222. It is reprinted with permission.

ALCOHOL ADDICTION: PRIESTS AND PRELATES

Joseph H. Fichter

*What is the role of the Bishop in
dealing with alcoholic priests? What if
he, himself, is alcoholic? Fichter
addresses these issues in this essay.*

Bishops who drink to excess are likely to be shielded by
associates and among the last to admit their own situation.
It is more comfortable to turn away from the problem, their
own and their priests'.

The official credo of the National Clergy Council on
Alcoholism concludes with the words: "We believe the
primary responsibility for implementing effective policies and
procedures for alleviating alcoholism lies with the leaders of
the family of God--our bishops." This responsibility for
promoting rehabilitation programs in industry, business
corporations, the military and elsewhere in work
organizations has been widely taken up by the leadership. It
has become apparent, as Paul Roman remarks, that "support
from top management can make or break a programming
effect," but church officials have been slow to give such
support.

Both the Episcopal Recovered Alcoholic Clergy
Association and the Catholic Clergy Council on Alcoholism
have sent copies of their programs and policies on
rehabilitation to their top church authorities. In 1971, Mark
Mindrup began an annual survey for N.C.C.A., sending
questionnaires to all the Catholic dioceses and male religious
orders. By 1976, only about one-fifth of them had
promulgated the program or were in the process of
formulating it. Even in these cases, there was often the
"tendency to regard the formulation of a written policy as
the creation of a program."

In a speech to the 1975 conference of the National Clergy Council on Alcoholism, John Keller, himself a clergyman and director of a rehabilitation unit, warned that "unless the president of the corporation makes a personal commitment and says we are going to do something about this--it is unrealistic to expect that anything significant is going to happen." In terms of the church, this means bishops and superiors, and the same principle applies. "If we have a bishop and we cannot get through to him, nothing can be done."

Bishop as Employer

Ordinarily, we do not think of the priest as employee and the bishop as employer, but, in any rational technical analysis of the diocesan structure, there can be no doubt that the bishop carries managerial authority and that the priest does his work subject to that authority. Vatican II's document Presbyterorum Ordinis says that priests, in their service to God and their fellow men, "dedicate their own wills through obedience." They are required to accept and carry out whatever is "commanded or recommended by their bishop."

The place where the priest works, the kind of work he does and the salary he receives are all fixed by the bishop, who also has the "management prerogative" of changing the work assignment and even of terminating the priest's employment. There is no such procedure as collective bargaining to determine issues like salary, hours and conditions of work, promotions, sick benefits, leaves of absences or vacations. The manner in which this relationship is carried out varies widely from diocese to diocese, but even where attempts have been made to implement the principles of subsidiarity and collegiality, there is no one in doubt that the bishop is the top employer, the ecclesiastical "boss."

The similarity between the company president and the diocesan ordinary is not quite so rigid as it may first appear. In the case of the alcoholic employee, there is a large difference in the manner in which sanctions are applied. The corporation executive can confront his worker with an ultimatum: "Either take treatment for your alcoholism or find yourself another job." The bishop on the other hand, knows that the alcoholic priest cannot find another job without leaving the priesthood. He may apply pressure, threaten to suspend the priest, to change his assignment or even to relieve him of it, but he is most reluctant to simply "fire" him. In the document *Christus Dominus*, Vatican II advises bishops to attend with "active mercy" upon priests who "have failed in some respect."

Captains of industry--and their personnel managers--are not necessarily without compassion and concern for the company employees, but if their business is to remain profitable they must be conscious of labor costs. It is commonly said (but with questionable empirical data) that billions of dollars are lost to the national economy every year because of absenteeism, accidents and shoddy work by alcoholic employees. Company management is also impressed by the fact that it costs money to replace trained and otherwise competent workers who are afflicted with alcoholism. It is good business policy, and less costly, to urge the worker to go through treatment for alcoholism and return to the job.

Perhaps this kind of monetary motivation is too crass for church officials who are reluctant to talk in economic terms of the employment relationship between bishop and priest. Yet, it has been put precisely in these terms: How much does it cost the diocese to educate a young man through the seminary until he is ready to take up priestly duties? In this sense, the diocese has an "investment" in its clergy personnel. If this young man turns out to be an alcoholic in later years, fails in his work assignment, perhaps causes scandal among the faithful, how much does it cost to rehabilitate him? Whatever other, and more important, values are involved, there is no question that there is also a cost-benefit value to the rehabilitation of alcoholic clergymen.

Bishop as Shepherd

No one calls a corporation president the "shepherd of his flock," but this biblical image is still sometimes applied to the Catholic bishop, who is expected to regard his priests as "sons and friends" and should always have a "special love," as well as a "trusting familiarity" for them. If the diocese is seen as a familial, or domestic, institution, rather than as a work organization, the fatherly authority of the bishop cannot be exercised in the same businesslike manner as is the authority of the company executive.

In the quaint language of biblical models and ecclesiastical lore, the pastoral care of the bishop is said to be much more extensive than the authority of the secular employer. He is supposed to have a personal solicitude about the "private life" of the priest, his spiritual welfare, his morale and even his bodily health. This is known as the **cura personalis**. The extent to which a bishop takes a personal interest in his priests depends only partly on his willingness and ability to do so. Our research has shown long ago that in the largest dioceses--some with over 1,000 priests--the bishop is not likely to exhibit this personal concern with frequency or intimacy.

This variation is demonstrated in the responses to questionnaires about alcohol rehabilitation sent to all the American dioceses. In the smaller places, the bishop himself answered the questionnaire; in the larger dioceses, it was usually the chancellor or some other diocesan official who did so. Similarly, when we asked who "handles" the problem priest, it was usually the bishop in the smaller dioceses who dealt with it personally. In the larger dioceses, it was a vicar for priests, and, less often, a special committee established for the clergy health and welfare.

Unless a bishop is an expert on alcoholism, or is himself a recovering alcoholic, he is probably not the best person to deal with the troubled priest. The conventional practice in the past was to keep the bishop in ignorance of the deviant clerical drinker, and many fellow clergy protected him, or "covered" for him. There remains in many places a distrust of the bishop, the feeling that the priest will be stigmatized if he is discovered, and that he will never be trusted again even if he takes treatment and maintains sobriety.

This problem of mutual distrust between priest and prelate is supposedly solved by the growing notion that alcoholism is a disease, and by the stipulation written into the diocesan rehabilitation program that no punitive action of any kind will be taken against the admitted alcoholic priest. Some of the recovering alcoholics we interviewed doubt whether bishops generally "really believe" that alcoholism is an illness. One rehabilitated man in a large diocese said "the bishop thinks we are saints because we have overcome a moral fault. He praises us to the skies, but, without realizing it, he treats us in a patronizing manner."

The typical American worker is resentful of paternalism on the part of his employer. He does not want the familial relationship of father to son, and does not believe that "father knows best" when it is a matter of his own conditions of work. Modern American priests--especially younger ones--are also reluctant to accept this familial concept. In place of the traditional direct and personal relationship with the bishop, many of them prefer now to deal with a diocesan personnel board, and, when necessary, with a grievance committee. The concepts of collegiality and coresponsibility, strongly supported by the Second Vatican Council, have lead in many places to the establishment of diocesan senates and clergy associations, and, on a broader scale, to the National Federation of Priests' Councils.

It is also at this point that the typical American employer-employee relationship breaks down again. The clergy are trained professionals in the full sense of the word, and the professional role differs significantly from that of the jobholder. In the complicated field of alcoholism rehabilitation, it is a well-known fact that people in the helping professions--physicians, teachers, lawyers, social workers, clergymen--are the most resistant to therapy. They tend, also, to be reluctant to admit to their professional colleagues, and to their supervisors or superiors, that they have succumbed to the "weakness" of alcohol addiction.

Bishop as Role Model

The Vatican II document Lumen Gentium tells us that bishops, "the shepherds of Christ's flock, ought to carry out their ministry with holiness, eagerness, humility and courage, in imitation of the eternal High Priest, the Shepherd and Guardian of our souls. They will thereby make this ministry the principal means of their own sanctification." In his letter to Titus, St. Paul had something to say about the elders and church leaders. "An elder must be without fault." After all, he is in charge of God's work, and "he must not be arrogant or quick-tempered, or a drunkard."

Paul certainly thought of the drunkard as a morally reprehensible person, and not as one who is afflicted with a serious illness. Experts in the field of alcoholism say it is a disease that has no respect of person or position. In a letter to the editor of America (6/11/77), Dr. James W. Brennan makes reference to alcoholic bishops who "are most reluctant to admit their problem and seek treatment." He remarks further that "those of us in the health field, however, are well aware that such bishops are no more immune to alcohol than are ordinary citizens, and do require rehabilitation."

What does it mean to be "more immune" or "less immune" to alcoholism? Spokesmen for N.C.C.A. frequently claim that the incidence of alcoholism is the same for clergymen as it is for American men in other occupations and professions. Some of the recovering clergy we interviewed did not hesitate to suggest that this generalization may be applied to members of the hierarchy as well as to the lower clergy. One of them revealed that the specific names of alcoholic bishops were submitted to the Vatican in the summer of 1973. This kind of document is, of course, a matter of the highest confidentiality, but when a bishop exhibits the telltale signs of alcoholism, he does not escape the eye of priests who have themselves gone through treatment and rehabilitation.

In the absence of data based on such close observation, one may merely speculate about the probable incidence of alcoholism in the Catholic hierarchy. A rough check of dates of ordination and consecration, as found in the Catholic Directory, shows that a man is, on the average, about 50 years of age when he is made a bishop. He has had sufficient time to prove himself a man of moderation and virtue, worthy of promotion, before he reaches this age in life. One supposes, also, that there has been a kind of screening process to eliminate potential alcoholics.

On the other hand, researchers in the field of alcoholism often point out that people of Irish descent constitute a "high risk" population for alcohol addiction. More than half of the diocesan ordinaries in the United States have Irish family names, but there is no way of telling how long ago their forebears came away from Ireland. Perhaps they come from a long line of Irish pioneers who were steadfast abstainers.

At any rate, the excessive drinkers in the hierarchy, and especially those who are alcoholics, are likely to be protected by the members of their official entourage, but there have been instances when this "cover" was broken through. There is an axiom among veterans in the field of rehabilitation that says that "the alcoholic is the first to know he has a problem, and the last to admit it," and this probably becomes more applicable the higher one ascends in the status structure. In a case of this kind, the question may well be asked, as it was at one convention of the National Clergy Council on Alcoholism: "If we have a bishop who has alcoholism, what are we going to do then?" One may answer that a bishop who is a recovered alcoholic could be most effective--provided Rome allows him to retain his office--in promoting a diocesan program of alcohol rehabilitation.

What To Do

This returns us to our starting point. The National Clergy Council on Alcoholism has been in existence for almost 30 years and is listed as an official "association" of the U.S. Catholic Conference. It has evolved a pragmatic program among church personnel and has distributed copies of this program to all dioceses in the United States. The key person to operationalize the program is the diocesan ordinary, the shepherd or ultimate employer of the clergy. There seem to be several reasons why the great majority of dioceses have not implemented the N.C.C.A. policy and program.

The first reason is that some bishops say that there is no problem of alcoholism among their priests, and they may well be right. The absolute dictum is questionable that there has to be a fixed percentage of clergy alcoholics in every diocese of the country. The fuzzy formula of 1-in-10, or 1-in-20 or whatever, is not universally applicable. In a small diocese where the alert bishop has close and frequent contact with his priests, it is an affront to his intelligence to say "he just doesn't know who the alcoholics are."

Another reason the bishop does not cooperate with the N.C.C.A. program is that he feels that excessive drinking is immoral and scandalous and should be kept quiet. This seems to be the case in one diocese, where the bishop had a reputation as a heavy drinker, if not an alcoholic. He quit abruptly, without going off for treatment, and sees no reason why everybody else cannot do the same. One of his priests said: "He has become so mean and irritable that I sometimes wish he'd go back to drinking."

A third reason that some bishops do not institute a program of alcohol rehabilitation is that they do not know how to proceed, or they are too busy about other diocesan matters. In more than one diocese, we were told: "The policy is all written up and has been sitting on the bishop's desk for over a year." Some bishops are simply not competent administrators, and, in a large diocese, are unable or unwilling to delegate authority to subordinates, including lay people, who know how to make the rehabilitation program work.

Finally, a drinking bishop may be reluctant to examine his own pattern of alcohol consumption. Dr. Russell Smith remarks that "none of us can approach alcoholism without getting emotionally involved," and this suggests that a close look at the alcoholic may demand that we take a close look at ourselves. Some members of N.C.C.A. say privately that the rehabilitation program is a "threat" to church officials who are themselves having trouble with booze. It is more comfortable just to turn away from the problem.

This article originally appeared in America 137.12 (1977): 258-260. It is reprinted with permission.

HELPING MY BROTHER PRIEST

Father Q.

*Father Q. explains how a priest can
help a fellow priest who is an alcoholic.*

The observations presented in this paper are not offered as a solution to the serious, baffling, complex problem of alcoholism. If I or anyone else could provide such a solution there would be no need for this [National Clergy Council on Alcoholism] Conference, nor for further research. Our objective here is to learn, if possible, the best methods of helping the alcoholic priest.

Can a priest help a fellow priest who is alcoholic? The answer is obviously yes, provided the one in need is willing to accept such help. The high office of the priest is to continue the mission of his Master, Christ. He must be all things to all men. He must feed the lambs and the sheep.

Potentially, any priest could help an alcoholic brother. But practically, the number of those who can render such assistance is limited, but not necessarily limited to those who are themselves alcoholic.

It must be remembered that in the case of the alcoholic priest there are three factors that must be considered in effecting his rehabilitation, restoring his sobriety, and setting him upon a firm foundation for maintaining it. First, there is the alcoholic priest himself. Second, there is the priest who extends the helping hand. Third, there is the bishop or superior. Each one of these must contribute certain essential elements if a happy conclusion is to be reached.

The alcoholic mind is one of frustrations, confusions, and fears. And by reason of his training intellectually and spiritually, they are exaggerated and distorted intensely and immensely in the priest's mind.

He fears lest his superior discover the fact of his excessive drinking, and to calm his fears he resorts to further drinking, seeking security in the oblivion of alcohol. He fears those around him and trusts nobody. Worst of all he fears God, and instead of turning to Him, he attempts to hide from Him.

It is pride, of course, but a terrible, devastating pride. A truly humble man need never fear. Such in brief is the alcoholic priest--he follows the pattern of all alcoholics.

The priest best qualified to help such a one, in my opinion, should be an established pastor, preferably without an assistant or assistants. If he himself is a recovered alcoholic, so much the better, provided he is deeply grateful to God for the gift of his own sobriety.

In any event, the helping priest must be filled with the charity of Christ and possessed of almost infinite patience, and he must be persistently ready to renew the struggle, even though his efforts repeatedly appear to be fruitless. He must never lose sight of the fact that he is dealing with a man who is dreadfully sick in heart and mind, in soul and body.

He must avoid any evidence of superiority, of looking down upon the object of his commiserations. His directions must be given by indirection. Without being in any way officious, he must make it possible for his subject to perform all the functions of his priestly office, insofar as circumstances permit.

At every opportunity he should direct conversations and discussions into channels that would emphasize the dignity of the priestly office and the consoling rewards for a ministry well spent. But all this must be a gradual process.

In the beginning it is enough if sobriety is accomplished. As this continues and becomes more established, the other elements of the spiritual life will be restored.

The first objective is to help the alcoholic acquire sobriety. Perhaps the most important fact to be gently driven home is that it is only for today, not for tomorrow, nor for a year, not for life--much less for eternity.

God gives life and He takes it away. We are all well aware of the truth that, if we live each moment that God gives us for God and according to His will, all will be with us here and hereafter.

All of our troubles result from endless worrying about the past and overanxiety about the future, neglecting the ever-present now. And all this is exaggerated beyond measure in the alcoholic. There is nothing complex about a true way of life.

The essence of the true spiritual life is to do now that which is in accord with the Will of God, that which is for our own good, and if circumstances require, that which is for the good of our neighbor. To restore that simplicity of the spiritual life in the alcoholic is a matter that requires time and more time, and the firm and kindly guidance of an understanding fellow-priest.

The alcoholic priest must not be required to center all his time and efforts upon his own rehabilitation. Quite the contrary. He more than anyone must exercise his charity towards others, not merely be an object of charity himself.

He must humble himself and the humble, and for that reason, it is all-important that he come in frequent contact with others who have the same problem as himself. He can help them and in doing he helps himself.

This demands that the priest who extends the helping hand must encourage him in this procedure, and in this, as in all phases of priestly activity, he must insist, if persuasion fails, that there be action.

The priest, following Christ, must spend himself in bringing sinners to repentance. There is no priest who can sit complacently on his cushioned chair in the rectory and accomplish this job with the effectiveness that Christ demands.

Though he has been made a sacred person through ordination, he must walk in the midst of sin, and must feel and touch its filth, yet be able to look upon its victim with pity and extend to him the mercy of forgiveness, if he is willing to receive it.

The alcoholic priest who sincerely desires to recover must, of necessity, be a **priestly** priest in order to be a good member of AA. Regardless of what individuals may have declared regarding the AA program, it demands perfection.

The flexibility of the program lies in the fact that the individual determines his way of life according to his understanding of God. The priest, therefore, cannot follow any slip-shod course. He must be another Christ, and if he is, he will draw others to Christ.

He must stand firmly for everything that the Church, the voice of God, demands in matters of faith and morals. His very stability and his clarity in expounding the correct principles of the spiritual side of the program will command the respectful attention of all, if he uses common sense and good judgment. He is, or he can be, the humble leader of the afflicted.

Briefly, the priest who undertakes to help another who is alcoholic must do his utmost to provide every means which may in any way effect a complete restoration of the ideals and practices of the priestly life.

What is required on the part of the ordinary or superior? It must be remembered that we refer throughout this discussion to the alcoholic priest who **wants** to quit drinking and who **seeks** assistance from another priest.

The bishop or superior must recognize his responsibility for his subject. He must look upon him as one of his sheep entrusted to him by Christ. I suppose it is only natural that many bishops and superiors feel that they themselves are **the goats** in having such sheep in their fold! Nevertheless the responsibility is theirs.

A bishop or superior desires before all else to continue to be a brother to other priests. Though the mantle of authority has been laid upon his shoulders, he does not wish that it be the predominant mark of his office.

He must be ever vigilant in insuring that the laws of God be respected and obeyed, but his constant prayer is that those precepts be observed from motivations of love rather than fear. This is his line of approach in dealing with any wayward subject.

In most instances he will gain more with gentle firmness than with penalties heartlessly imposed. A bishop or superior can never effect any benefit for an alcoholic priest unless he can win his confidence and trust.

Severity, censure, confinement in some ecclesiastical institution--any of all of these are utterly ineffective. Such procedure merely arouses greater resentment, deeper fear and mistrust, with the result that the object of it turns to the bottle in desperation.

No one heaps greater condemnation and rebuke upon the alcoholic priest than he does himself; but he rebels when such judgment comes from his superior. When a priest undertakes to help his alcoholic brother, the bishop or superior must give him the fullest cooperation.

He should lift all censures and penalties; he should place no limitation on his subject, so far as the exercise of the ministry is concerned, while he is in the process of rehabilitation, under the supervision of a fellow priest; and, finally, he must insure that once rehabilitated, his subject will be given a chance to exercise his sacerdotal powers under conditions best suited to maintain his sobriety.

Not all alcoholic priests can be rehabilitated through the help of other priests alone. Many will need other forms of treatment and therapy. But whatever the condition may be, the wise and kindly and complete cooperation of bishops and superiors, with those who have the know-how of the recovery of alcoholics, is necessary. God will not be wanting to their needs.

This article originally appeared in Alcoholism. Indianapolis: National Clergy Council on Alcoholism, 1960. It is reprinted with permission.

AFTERCARE: IN THE RELIGIOUS COMMUNITY

Sister Maurice Doody, O.P.

Alcoholism is a family disease and the religious community is no less family than the alcoholic's biological family. Doody explains family dynamics in terms of religious communities.

"And the King will answer, 'I tell you solemnly, in so far as you did this to one of the least of mine, you did it to me'" (Mt 25:40-41).

Recovery from chemical dependency is a process and the road to recovery is not an easy one; it is not a straight one. There are many curves, detours, and steep inclines. It is a road filled with disillusionment and dismay. Personal recovery is a process rather than a completed even, because it is ongoing as a style of life. Recovery involves the whole person, the physical being, the psychological-emotional being and the spiritual being. The real test of recovery comes in everyday living, living one's life in society, chemically free.

The community, particulary the local community, has various expectations about the recovering chemically dependent person. Sometimes these expectations can cause a tremendous amount of anxiety and stress. The dependent persons are eager to put into practice the tools for sobriety they have learned but at the same time they may be anxious about relapse (which is symptomatic of this illness as it is with other illnesses), a job, the attitude of the community, the attitude of friends and relatives. They are concerned with how long before things fall in place.

Relatives, friends, co-workers, and members of the community wonder about such things as: Are they going to drink or use again? Are they angry with us for forcing them into treatment? What should we expect, not that they are not drinking or using? Should we keep alcohol in the house? Will they be upset if we drink?

Aftercare provides a bridge from treatment back to so-called "normal living" for both the patients and the community. The adjustment period is equally crucial for the community members. The "walking-on-eggs" feeling can be diminished when talking and sharing with others take place. Community members will experience some difficulty in establishing a new way of life. Too long their normal reactions and feelings have been disguised. The "don't-talk-about-it-rule" has to be lifted. The techniques of "letting go" and not attempting to change or control the chemically dependent persons have to begin. Community members must work through their resentments. They must move from feelings of antagonism, confusion, pain, skepticism, and disbelief into building a healthy life not dependent on the behavior or progress of the chemically dependent persons.

The community can make the job of maintaining sobriety either easier or more difficult depending on whether it provides an atmosphere which facilitates recovery or one which works against the chances of success. Persons who have spent years of getting their mental processes confused will not straighten out the situation by experiencing one momentary flash of self-honesty. Permanent restoration will require continued effort, plus the patient, understanding help of those who can tolerate occasional slips without losing patience with the long range process. It is extremely important that the local community come to the realization that we are not dealing with appendicitis but rather with a very insidious illness.

The community can help by developing greater awareness and understanding of the nature of the illness since after the intensive treatment phase, the concerned community is involved in the remainder of the recovery process. Knowledge and changed attitudes on the part of the community will assure that the dependent persons receive the same consideration and respect as those with other illnesses and problems.

Whether a person has spent time in a treatment facility or has become involved in a program of recovery, having a chemical dependency counselor or having someone trained in the area of chemical dependency meet with the local community can help to develop empathic understanding of what will have to be done to continue the recovery process. At such a meeting the community would be prepared for their supportive role by realizing the amount of time and effort recovery will require. In the recovery process, time spent in a treatment facility is about ten percent of getting well. This is the time to break the addictive cycle. It is believed that it takes from two-to-three years of recovery before the central nervous system returns to basically normal functioning. Too often the chemically dependent persons who have been in a treatment facility or have been to a few AA meetings are thought of as being "cured" or "not cured." These two concepts are incorrect and inaccurate. They are potentially destructive because the chemically dependent persons need time to get well. The body, mind, and spirit heal slowly.

Changes in the attitude and the behavior of the community can facilitate recovery, but the community cannot do the recovering for the dependent persons. The community may have gotten along without them so, when they return, there may be conscious, as well as unconscious, resistance to accepting them as responsible members and to returning their role or place back to them. There may be a great many hostile feelings relating to the chemical experience, sometimes on the surface and sometimes hidden very deep. The recovering persons will be changing, and this will mean changing relationships with others. Having a sober individual rather than an intoxicated one to deal with is as major a change as having one who behaves responsibly rather than irresponsibly.

The community may expect the dependent persons to be "fixed" after treatment and be as they remember them before they became chemically dependent. In actuality they may return home very nervous and impatient, having feelings of guilt, remorse, and inadequacy. The community may fear that they will slip back into using their drug or drugs of choice and so they tend to mind them. What seems to be needed, mostly, is a warm, human concern. Communication is essential at this time in order for all to recover--both the afflicted and the affected. It is extremely important that the dependent persons and those associated with them get in touch with their feelings, talk about their sadness, anger, frustration, fear, and hostility. This can be accomplished for the chemically dependent persons in the AA program and, if necessary, with counseling as a supplement to AA. The local community can find assistance in the Al-Anon program and/or a chemical dependency counselor.

Dr. Gordon Bell, in talking about the recovering person, stated: "They must find new dependence on unused resources within themselves, on other people, and on the powers that transcend people altogether." It is hoped that communities will try to create an atmosphere in which this "new dependence" can take place. The message that should be coming through loud and clear from the community at large, the local community, and the significant others in the chemically dependent persons' lives is one of support: **We cannot do it for you but we will walk with you.**

The article originally appeared in Sisters Today (April, 1981): 480-482. Reprinted with permission of the author.

For Further Reading on
Alcoholic Clergy and Women Religious

Anonymous (1989). My Skid Row Was My Convent Room. Park Ridge, Illinois: Parkside Medical Corporation.

This pamphlet tells the story of Mary Rachel Cloonan, an alcoholic nun. Special emphasis is placed on how denial kept others from confronting her about her problem and how her community reacted to her addiction and recovery. General information on alcoholic clergy is also given.

Bissell, L., & Haberman, P. W. (1984). Alcoholism in the Professions. New York: Oxford University Press.

Although not a focus of the study, Bissell and Haberman briefly describe various denominations' responses to alcoholic clergy. It is, however, a good resource for understanding the needs of professionals.

Doody, M. (August/September 1978). Chemical Dependency. Sisters Today, 24-31.

Doody discusses chemical dependency in the religious community and encourages community members to do an intervention with the dependent sister. She defines chemical dependency, social drinking, symptoms of addiction, intervention, and recovery.

Dooher, G. B. (1987). Chemical Dependency Among Religious Ministers. Human Development, 8(2), 7-13.

Dooher describes how physical health is affected by alcoholism, how to recognize chemical dependency, and how to conduct an intervention. The types of treatment programs available for alcoholic ministers are also described.

Fichter, J. (1977). Alcohol and Addiction: Priests and Prelates.

Royce, J. E. (1987). Alcohol and Other Drugs in Spiritual Formation. Studies in Formative Spirituality, 6(2), 211-222.

Fr. Royce writes about the problem of addiction among priests and nuns and how addiction adversely affects religious development. The role of AA in helping to promote spirituality in recovery is emphasized.

Sammon, S. (1989). Alcoholism's Children: ACoAs in Priesthood and Religious Life. Staten Island, New York: Alba House.

Sammon describes how being an adult child of an alcoholic affects the religious vocations of priests, nuns and brothers. Family roles are emphasized as is recovery from these roles.

Smith, R. F. The Guest House Story. National Convention of Catholic Physicians. Kansas City, Missouri.

Smith gives a history of Guest House giving special attention to changing attitudes about alcoholic clergy.

Sorenson, A. A. (1976). Alcoholic Priests: A Sociological Study. New York: Seabury Press.

Sorenson compares drinking among British and American priests, family background of alcoholic clergy, and the drinking and vocational careers of alcoholic priests. Both Catholic and Episcopalian priests are studied.

INDEX